Character Curriculum fc

Hope Chest Series
Volume 2

Preparing Your Hope Chest

By Mrs. A. B. Leaver

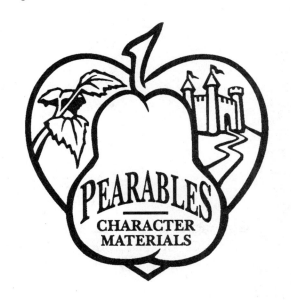

PEARABLES
CHARACTER
MATERIALS

This book is dedicated to the future mothers in Christ.

Special thanks to Anna and Autumn.

...Also to Grandmother who lived out everything in this book!

Introduction

It is with our utmost thankfulness to God, that we have been able to produce for you, <u>Preparing Your Hope Chest</u> for young Christian ladies of today.

Our own daughters are also being prepared for that most honored station of home-making. Because of this, we decided to print a book written, not for mothers, but specifically for these precious daughters.

We have tried to make the format itself daughter friendly. We have struggled with trying to make our own young ladies read through thick, endless books of miniature squiggles. Even though mother may think a book is fabulous and skim quickly through the small fonts and print, many young girls get overwhelmed at tiny print and pictureless pages.

<u>Preparing Your Hope Chest</u> is just for them! We pray it will encourage the daughters in your family and teach them how to find a hope chest that will meet their needs. Then it will tell them exactly what a hope chest was for in the past and the importance of having one today in a young female life. It will be a tool that will help you prepare your loved one for her duties as a homemaker.

We hope that each skill accomplished will only whet her appetite for more womanly arts and talents!

How to use this book:

~It works best as a mother/daughter journey into the fascinating preparation for Christian womanhood.

~Please do not set a time limit for each project. Some skills take longer to acquire than others. Daughters should try to complete a project and if mother thinks it still needs to be worked on, should gently suggest making another one. Hint: Try not to ever say that their work is not up to par, as that may discourage their young hearts. Ask them to make another one for a family member, and then help them in the areas where they are lacking. Concentrate on helping them perfect their skill.

~Once the book is completed, go to your local library and continue to find projects for your daughters to keep working on.

Mothers, this book isn't the end of the journey. It's just a tool to scratch the surface!

Our prayers are with you as you start this feminine project. It will be a wonderful time of fellowship with the other young females in your life.

Maranatha,

Mrs. A. B. Leaver & Friends

Index

Chapter	PAGE
I. Preparing Your Hope Chest	8
II. How to Find Your Own Hope Chest	14
a. Places to Find Inexpensive Hope Chests	16
b. Refinishing an Old Hope Chest or New Wood	17
III. Deciding What Skills You will Need	20
a. Your Career Preparation (for home)	20
b. Making Your own Handiwork Bag	24
IV. Handiwork	32
a. Crotchet	34
b. Knitting	36
c. Short & Sweet Knit Scarf	41
V. Embroidery	44
a. Step by Step Decorative Stitches	46
b. Handkerchief Embroidery	50
VI. Sewing	54
a. Stocking Your Sewing Basket	56
b. Making a Hand-Sewn Baby Quilt	58
c. The Sewing Machine	62

VII. **Decorating Skills**   64
    a. Keep it Simple   65
    b. Stenciling   67
    c. Framing Greeting Cards   72

VIII. **Kitchen Preparation**   76
    a. Check List   78
    b. Aluminum Poisoning   80
    c. Lead Poisoning   81
    d. The China Syndrome   82
    e. Finding Your Linens   84

IX. **Cooking**   86
    a. Studying Good Nutrition   88
    b. Vitamin Deficiencies and Signs of Excess   90
    c. Collecting Your Recipe Notebook   95
    d. Recipe Pattern   97
    e. Recipes to Cut Out   99
    f. Categorizing Your Notebook   118

X. **House Cleaning**   120
    a. Do Not Clutter Your Home   121
    b. Cleaning Chart   122
    c. Cleaning List   123
    d. Cleansers   124
    e. Vacuum   127
    f. Stain Removal Tips   128
    g. Preparing for Housework   130

XI. **Frugality**   132

    a. You Do Not Make More Money Working   134

    b. Being a Mother to Your Children at Home   135

    c. Start a Frugal Notebook   136

    d. Frugal Shopping Tips   137

    e. Homemade Mixes   140

    f. Being Frugal with Money   144

    g. Frugal Entertainment   145

XII. **Not the End of the Story**   150

    a. More Ideas   152

Resources   156

CHAPTER ONE

⟶ Preparing Your Hope Chest ⟵

What is a hope chest?

In our culture and also in some European countries, it was customary for young, unmarried daughters to prepare a chest in hopes of being married one day.

I'm sure that you, too, dream of marrying and having your own family. This is what God has intended for most young women.

Unfortunately, the modern unchristian world of today does not prepare young women for marriage. Rather, they teach that having a career is the most important pursuit for young women and men. They believe that a hope chest is for collecting home items and that this is "preparing" for marriage.

Why don't you stop reading right now, and before you continue on, think of what you believe a hope chest is.

Now, do you have your thoughts? Then let's read again and find out what modern society thinks a hope chest is vs. what the truth about them are.

The following are modern day false myths:

~A hope chest is for collecting china.
~A hope chest is where you store all your expensive linens & silver.
~A hope chest is where you place all of your belongings for when you get married.
~A hope chest is where you place your trousseau.
~A hope chest is where you place all of your heirlooms.
~A hope chest must be made out of cedar.

Now, how many of your ideas were the ones listed under myths? If you thought most of these things, you are not alone! Ninety nine per cent of American society believes these thoughts regarding hope chests.

Let's view again the list regarding today's myths and expound a bit.

~A hope chest is for collecting china.

A hope chest was not a collection box. China dishes were only for the very, very wealthy, and still is! You could plan on spending around $1,000 on a full china service to serve eight people. This is probably the least expensive of sets. Some dishes are *$58 a piece*!

In our American past, when traveling, a young lady of moderate means would have found all her china broken after it arrived at the home of her new husband, unless it was packed in a china trunk.

~A hope chest is where you store all your expensive linens & silver.

Again, only the very wealthy would purchase silver dinnerware. These people would also have had their silver stored in locked trunks.

Today, the best silverware to purchase would be stainless steel, and very nice sets can be found inexpensively at garage or estate sales.

You would place your silverware in a box with your pots and pans, but that will be discussed later on.

~A hope chest is where you place all of your belongings for when you get married.

No, your hope chest is not a suitcase.

Many people who were not brought up with having a hope chest have misconceived ideas that everything you see around you that you would like to have for your future home is to be stored in your chest.

The reality of it is that you will most likely have ten times the amount of belongings and it would not fit inside the chest.

It always bothered me as a young lady to even think of preparing a hope chest because I knew that when I looked at my mother's home, all the items she needed would definitely not fit inside. It seemed a waste of time to only place a few items in the chest.

When I discussed this with my best friend, she told me that it was a place where you put your kitchen items for when you were married.

Well, I scratched my head and thought about that for a long time and didn't even think that the kitchen items would fit in the trunk!

So what WAS a hope chest for????

~A hope chest is where you place your trousseau.

A trousseau is what they used to call the bride's possessions. It usually consisted of her clothes, accessories and household linens and wares.

According to Stanley's 1769 Ladies Book, the lady's trousseau was stored in many chests for travel. Her belongings, once again, took up much more space than one singular hope chest.

~A hope chest is where you place all of your heirlooms.

I have heard of young women using their hope chests as storage places for beloved heirlooms. But this is not what usually went into one in the past, unless the item would be used for instructional help regarding homemaking in the future.

And last, but not least:

~A hope chest must be made out of cedar.

Cedar was often preferred because it would naturally keep out moths, as moths abhor cedar. This would keep all linen items safe from harm.

There are many old chests which are made out of all types of wood.

As you will see from reading on, we will be finishing one which is made from pine wood and purchased from Hobby Lobby, or some other craft store.

✿✿✿✿✿✿✿✿✿✿✿✿✿✿✿✿✿✿

So now that we know what hope chests are not, what were they? Why did families consider it so important that each daughter have one?

Hope Chests Were Tools to Show Skills Completed & Lessons Learned in Preparation For Marriage

In other words, a hope chest was used by parents to teach their daughters the necessary skills needed for running a home when they had one of their own.

Hope chests were one of the most wonderful tools ever created to bring mother and daughter close together in womanly fellowship.

It was mother's duty to make sure that her precious daughters were well equipped with all the knowledge they would need in order to care well for their own husbands and children.

To do this, she would make a list of certain items for her daughters to accomplish. Once the list was made, mother would then proceed in teaching the young ladies, one skill at a time.

Once the skill was obtained, and an item was completed to the mother's satisfaction, this carefully completed keepsake and household item was then added to the hope chest. Not only would it be a functional piece of houseware, it would also be the graduation trophy to show that all skills needed had been reached and accomplished. The young lady was now skilled with the special art of homemaking in that area and was now ready to tackle another!

The completed hope chest was the sign that a young lady was now ready for marriage.

Are you being prepared for marriage? Do you think that running a household is something that we just fall into?

Unlike the world who does not know Christ, we are to learn to walk in the ways of the Lord as young women. God has given us a glorious duty in womankind. There is so much joy in a job well done. When we view our duties as women in the light that they are skills that we have learned and we do them well, our attitude will reflect the happiness that is within us. Being a woman in the Lord is one of the most rewarding existences on the face of the earth.

Each day will bring you new adventures in creativity that you may have never even knew existed! Why, God creates. God is the Master Creator. When we were created by Him, He created us in His image. We also create. Homemaking and developing womanly skills is also how we as women create. Through God's help, we will create a home from a house. We will create meals from groceries; linens, curtains and clothing from material! The possibilities are endless!

The following chapters are to give you just a glimpse into the skills needed to maintain and run your own home some day. We will start with the very basic skills. Then it is up to you and your mother to continue in perfecting these womanly arts.

When your hope chest is completed, then you know you are on your way to being prepared to be a wife and mother!

❇❇❇❇❇❇❇❇❇❇❇❇❇❇

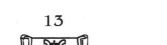

Photos of Lane cedar chests.

CHAPTER TWO

How To Find Your Own Hope Chest

Searching for a hope chest is a wonderful thing to do with your mother or grandmother. Many fathers are also starting to participate in the purchase of a hope chest.

There is one special company which has been around for a very long time. My mother told the story of when graduation came around, in her small coastal town, Lane Furniture Company gave a small, pencil-box size, free, cedar chest to each girl who graduated. It was still the norm that most young women would be having a family and would be homemakers; so it was an incentive to go to the best cedar chest makers in the country! They are still around today.

You can purchase one of their chests for about $300 on up, and the number to find them is below. If your family can afford them, they are a purchase well worth every penny!

LANE Hope Chests:
1-800-750-LANE

Places to Find Inexpensive Hope Chests

There are many young ladies whose fathers are the sole provider for their families, and their mothers, thankfully, are staying at home with the children. It may be difficult for the traditional family to find the money to purchase one of the more expensive chests.

Don't let that deter you! There are many ways in which the Lord has provided daughters with a hope chest.

~Garage sales. As you will find throughout this book, we are solid advocates of garage sales. We know of many dear friends who have found the perfect hope chest for under $75 at a garage sale.

~Flea markets. In our town we have a local flea market every weekend which is held in an old warehouse. Two of our friends came upon treasures there. Both found the perfect cedar chest!

~Antique stores. The cedar chests found at antique stores are usually a bit more expensive than those that you might find at a garage sale or flea market. Unless they are really old, they are usually cheaper than the new ones.

~Estate sales. An estate sale is a sale which is held after someone has passed away. We have found beautiful hope chests that someone lovingly cherished, and I'm sure that they would be so happy to know that their cedar chest has found a new home.

If you are unable to find a hope chest within your means, you may wish to find one that is already made, but in raw wood form. We found one which was only $95 at Hobby Lobby. It was called a "boot box", but it served our purpose as a hope chest just fine! (They did have larger hope chests, but they were about $150).

~Read the next portion first, before you buy your supplies.

Refinishing an Old Hope Chest or Starting With Raw Wood

The following hope chest was found at Hobby Lobby. Actually, they called it a "Boot Chest", but it was a hope chest to us!

A boot chest turned hope chest in raw pine.

What you will need:

~ Garnet Sandpaper 320 grit
~ Minwax Polyshades 1 Quart
~ Minwax Pre-Stain Conditioner
~ 2 1/2" Touch-up Brush
~ Plastic Gloves for staining

Finishing Your Hope Chest

1. Purchase GARNET SANDPAPER, super fine. ACE hardware has a wonderful selection and the people are personal and very helpful.   When working with soft pine, you must use the finest sandpaper you can find. If you use a coarser grade, your hope chest will have lines and scratch marks. If you have found a harder type of wood, you can use fine grit. Try a corner first, on the bottom. Sand in delicate circles. If you get a smooth surface with no scratches you are ready to go!

Sand everything. The inside, outside and bottom. You might wish to wear a dust mask as it is not good to inhale the wood particles.

2. Next, take a towel rag and thoroughly wipe off all remaining dust that is left on the hope chest.

You are now ready for staining!

3. <u>Minwax Pre-stain Conditioner</u>. Follow the directions on the back of your can. Within two hours you must use the Minwax Polyshades for staining.

4. Choosing your color. We used MINWAX POLYSHADES, which is stain & Polyurethane in one-step.

For those of you who do not know what stain is, stain is the color you are going to make your hope chest.

Polyurethane is the gloss which protects your wood from damage. In the past you had to do two steps, first stain and then polyurethane. Now, thanks to Minwax Polyshades, it is only one procedure!

We chose Pecan Gloss 420, which is a medium stain. They recommended 2 1/2" touch-up brushes.

<u>Put on your gloves</u>. <u>Paint on your stain/gloss solution, not missing any areas. Let dry thoroughly and then apply a second coat.</u>

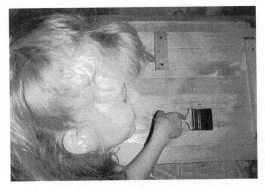

You are now ready to prepare to fill your beautiful hope chest. This item will become a family heirloom that will be passed down for generations.

CHAPTER THREE

Deciding What
∽ *Skills You Will Need* ∽

*"Teach the young women to be ... discreet,
chaste, <u>keepers at home</u>."
Titus 2:5*

Do you remember what the purpose of a hope chest is? It is a tool used by parents to help train their daughters in homemaking preparation.

Your Career Preparation
(Being a Keeper At Home)

The highest career calling that a young lady has is that of wife and mother. The Scriptures tell us:

That the older women (mothers and grandmothers) are to teach the younger women (their daughters and granddaughters) to "...love their husbands, to love their children, to be discreet, chaste, keepers at home, i.e., **homemakers**, good, obedient to their own husbands, that the Word of God may not be blasphemed." Titus 2:3-5

Many young women are being taught to have careers outside of the home. They are being trained to be secretaries, writers, doctors, nurses, business owners, lawyers, etc. Their education is so full of humanistic training that they have neglected the Scriptural teachings of what the Bible says a daughter is to be taught.
Many marriages of today end in divorce because daughters are not being trained to love their husbands or their children. They are

not being taught to be a homemaker, but rather to have occupations *outside* the home.

The most wonderful career for a woman to have is that of homemaker. But every career needs careful supervision and training. Would you go to a doctor who had not been trained in his skill? Would you go to a dentist who had never been trained in dentistry? It would be a bit scary!

It is very frightening to think of young men today marrying young ladies who have not been taught the skills necessary for their careers!

Can you imagine the chaos that follows when a man would marry a woman simply because she looks pretty on the outside? Her looks will fail, and soon she will become old and no longer pretty on the outside. What will happen when he finds out that she cannot take care of a home? When he comes home and clothes are thrown around on the floor? The kitchen is a disaster because no one has cleaned it? When she demands to be taken out to dinner every day because she doesn't know how to cook? The young man will find that he has entered a nightmare of horrific proportions!

There have been many stories told where the lady was not taught any homemaking skills and disaster followed.

For example, there was a young couple who had been married for about a year. The wife had never been taught to clean, cook, organize, to be frugal, or any homemaking skills at all. The only things she knew to buy were frozen meals and cereal. She had never been taught how to clean anything, and soon dirt accumulated.

The problem only accelerated when their first child came. She hadn't known how to care for a baby. She didn't change the diapers as she should, and the baby developed terrible sores all over his bottom. She didn't change the baby's sheets, and the baby became ill. The hospital informed social services and they went to check the home. Because the home was so filthy, they took the baby away from the mother and declared the parents unfit to care for the child.

This is a very sad but true story, and it has happened to hundreds of thousands of parents across the nation.

But to those of us in Christ, we have a wonderful handbook to follow: the Bible! The Bible tells us that we are to be taught skills for our career, homemaking! This is what the hope chest is all about.

As Christians, we know that homemaking is our main career choice, but what should our course of study be?

With every career you must study, and you are given a syllabus of which courses you will take.

It is the same with our career! Homemaking!

The following skills are just the tip of the iceberg. There are many more which you will find as you enter this wonderful realm of homemaking which are not listed.

~Handiwork
     ~Crochet
     ~Knitting
     ~Embroidery

~Sewing
     ~Stocking your sewing basket
     ~How to sew
     ~Mending

~Decorating skills, to make a house a home.
     ~Cross Stitch
     ~Ruffles
     ~Making your own curtains

~Preparing for your kitchen.

~Cooking and recipes.

~How to prepare bedrooms.

~*How to prepare bathrooms.*

~*Preparing your home office.*

~*Cleaning skills.*

~*Being frugal and budgeting.*

~*Gardening.*

~*Preparing for your first baby.*

We will be covering some of these topics, but it is up to you to go further once this book is finished. But warning! Once you get started, you are never going to want to stop! ☺

In order to begin, we must have the tools that we are going to use. The first items we will be making will be a handiwork bag, and sewing kit.

You can purchase both of these at sewing stores, but we found them to be expensive. For example, a sewing kit that is of a large size (over 12" in diameter) begins at $49. The ones that were very nice cost $90 each!

As a homemaker, the first thing to remember is that most of the time, you can make all the things that you see for a fraction of the price that you could buy them. The only thing you spend is your time and elbow grease!

Making & Designing your own Handiwork Bag

What you will need to make a handiwork bag:

~ A plain canvas bag $2
~ Permanent fabric paint
(3 in pckg. = $3

~ Stencils $2 each

~ Pencil

1. Iron your bag so that it is flat with no wrinkles or puckers.

2. Take a pencil and stencil your design on your bag.

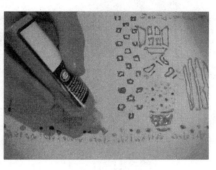

3. Take your fabric paint and carefully finish coloring your stenciled design.

Here is the finished product!

You are ready to carry whatever project you are working on, wherever you may go.

These canvas bags with fabric paint can be washed and ironed over and over!

Making Your own Sewing Kit

What you will need:

~ A wicker basket with a handle that folds up. We found ours at Walmart: one for $2.97 and the other, a bit larger, for $4.97.

~ 3 yards fabric, cotton, upholstery or satin, of your choice.

~ Batting for quilts.

~ 3 yards ribbon to match fabric.

~ 3 yards of lace for edging.

~ Cardboard Boxes.

~ Crafting glue.

~ Measuring tape.

~ Scissors.

1. Measure from bottom center of basket to the largest outer corner. Our smallest basket measured 12". Multiply that by two. You need to cut a circle the exact inches of the product. Ours, for example, was 48" in diameter.

2. Next, take basket and trace around bottom onto a piece of cardboard. The side of a cardboard box works great!

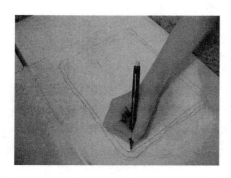

3. After you have traced the bottom, make a line 1/2 inch smaller inside this one. Cut out, using the *smaller* pattern. This will be the bottom for the inside of the sewing box.

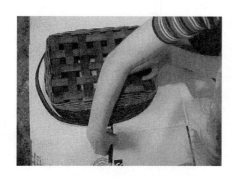

4. Place basket upside down on cardboard and trace around outside edge. Be exact. The cardboard you are making will be the lid of your sewing basket, so be careful that they are the same size. Cut 2 of these.

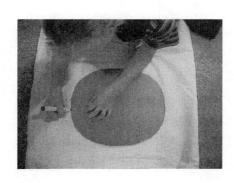

5. Next, take your cardboard lid and your cardboard bottom and place it on fabric. We are using contrasting pieces. You will need 2 of these for the lid and one for the bottom. Trace with a light marker around the edge on your material.

Note: You will have 2 pieces of material for the top. One for the bottom.

6. Now make another line, all the way around this trace mark, 4 inches out.

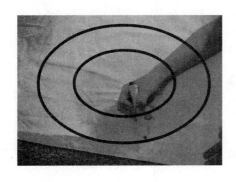

7. Do this also with the bottom cardboard piece. See Note above.

8. Take your material and place your basket in the center. Pull the material up even on each side of the handles. Pin to mark the top edge of the basket. Cut a straight line where each of your handles will go. Let material lay flat but line cuts up with handles.

9. Take glue and glue all inside the basket.

10. Now, evenly pull all the edges and bring them to the center of the inside of the basket. Press so that glue sticks to fabric.

11. Take your bottom piece of cardboard. You need to cut a piece of batting the same size.

12. Take the batting and glue it to one side of the bottom cardboard piece.

13. Take your material and pull smoothly over the cardboard with batting. Turn over the cardboard and glue the edges of the material on the wrong side. This is the bottom of your sewing basket.

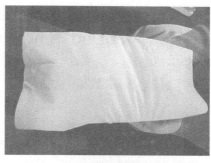

14. Glue this bottom into the bottom of your sewing kit. Press firmly until dry.

The Lid:

15. Take your cardboard and cut a piece of batting the same size as the lid.

16. Take one of the pieces of lid patterns and pull tight. Glue on opposite side. Glue on cardboard.

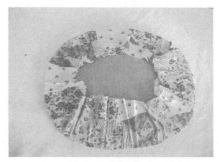

17. Take the other cardboard lid and do the same as #16. *Only, do not put batting on this one.*

18. Glue lace around the outside edge of the one without the batting.

19. Glue unfinished sides together. Your lid is now ready for attachment.

20. Take two pieces of ribbon 2 inches long. On the inside of the sewing kit, attach with glue one end of the ribbon. Cut 2 pieces of ribbon 8 inches long for the latch bow. Glue one to the top and one to the bottom. Let dry.

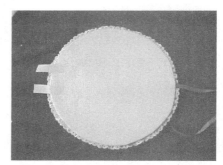

21. Now attach the lid pieces. Let dry with lid on sewing kit.

Finishing touches:

21. **Decorating the Handles.** You can do this before you attach the lid, or after. It doesn't really matter. Take one end of ribbon and glue it to the bottom of one side of the handle. Wrap the whole handle. If you would like, you can use another complimentary color and space wrap again! Add bows as much as you like!

Voila!   The finished product.

A hand knitted sweater

CHAPTER FOUR

❧ *Handiwork* ❧

> *"She seeks wool and flax, and **willingly** works with her hands."*
> *Proverbs 31:13*

Handiwork means just what the word implies. It is working with your hands to create or fix something.

There is something so wonderfully satisfying when you have created an object with your hands, and stand back, and like what you have done.

Our Heavenly Father did this when He created the earth and all that was within it. He stood back and saw, "that it was good". (Genesis 1:31)

Each day we have a choice. We can live in idleness and only pleasure ourselves, or we can actually make our day worthwhile and get something done.

Many great-grandmothers of today still believe that your hands should not be idle. I've seen many older women at Bible studies and at family gatherings knitting away in a comfy corner, while everyone visits together. During this "visiting" time, they have completed hundreds of knitting or crotcheting projects over the years!

They hold the belief that idle hands is the beginning towards the highway of a sinful, selfish life.

As a young lady who is preparing her hope chest, we are going to teach you some valuable skills so you will never find your hands idle.

The first skill we are going to be working on is learning to crotchet.

We would like to thank the <u>Craft Yarn Council of America</u> who helped us with the following projects. For more information and help you can go to their web page at: www.learntoknit.com

Crotchet

Beginners Single Crochet Dishcloth

This pattern uses only single crochet.

What you need:

- Worsted-weight yarn, any color or colors
- Size G crochet hook;
- Yarn needle with big eye
- Small scissors How to begin

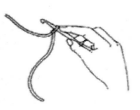

Step 1: Hold crochet hook in right hand and make a slip knot on hook.

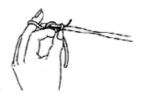

Step 2: Bring yarn over hook from back to front and grab it with hook.

onechain stitch

Step 3: Draw hooked yarn through slip knot and onto hook. This makes one chain stitch.

Repeat Steps 2 and 3 in sequence 28 more times. You should have 29 chain stitches and one loop will remain on hook.

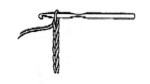

Step 4: Skip the first chain stitch.

Step 5: Insert hook into center of next chain stitch. Draw yarn through the chain stitch and up onto the hook. There are now 2 loops on hook.

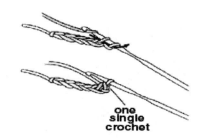

one single crochet

Step 6: Bring yarn over hook from back to front, and draw it through both loops on hook. One loop remains on the hook, and you have just made one single crochet stitch.

Repeat Steps 5 and 6 in each of the remaining 27 chains--be sure to work in the very last chain. You have now completed one row of single crochet. Measure your work; it should be about 7" wide. If it is too wide, try again with fewer beginning chains. If it is too narrow, try again with more beginning chains.

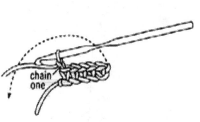

chain one

Step 7: At the end of the row, make one chain stitch, then turn the work counterclockwise, leaving the hook in the chain.

Now you can begin another row, working into the stitches of the previous row.

Step 8: Make one single crochet stitch in first stitch and in each remaining stitch of the previous row. Be sure to work into the last stitch. Chain 1, turn.

Repeat Step 8 until the block measures 9" long.

Finishing: Cut the yarn from the skein, leaving a 6" end. Draw the hook straight up, bringing the yarn through the remaining loop on the hook.

Knitting
Beginner Doll Blanket

What you need:

- Worsted-weight yarn, any color or colors
- Size 8, 14"-long knitting needles

- Yarn needle with big eye
- Small scissors

Casting On

Step 1: Make a slip knot on the shaft of one needle. This counts as your first stitch.

Step 2: Place this needle in left hand. Hold other needle in right hand to control the yarn. Insert point of right needle, from front to

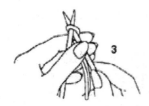

back, into the slip knot and under the left needle.

Step 3: Hold left needle still in left hand, and move left fingers over to brace right needle.

Step 4: With right index finger, pick up the yarn from the ball.

Step 5: Release right hand's grip on the needle, and use index finger to bring yarn under and over the point of right needle.

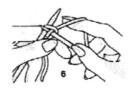

Step 6: Return right fingers to right needle, and draw yarn through stitch with point of right needle.

Step 7: Slide point of left needle into back of new stitch, then remove right needle.

Step 8: Pull ball yarn gently to make the stitch fit snuggly on needle. You have now made one stitch (called casting on), and there

are two stitches on left needle (slip knot is counted as a stitch).

Step 9: Insert point of right needle, from front to back, into stitch just made, and under left needle. Repeat Steps 5 through 9, 26 more times, until you have 28 stitches on the left needle. This completes the cast-on row, which is the way all knitting is begun.

First Knit Row
Step 1: Hold needle with stitches in left hand; insert point of right needle in first stitch, from front to back, just as in casting on.

Step 2: With right index finger, bring yarn from ball under and over point of right needle.

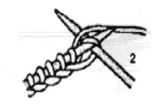

Step 3: Draw yarn through stitch with right needle point.

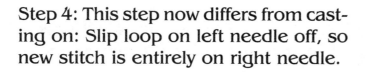

Step 4: This step now differs from casting on: Slip loop on left needle off, so new stitch is entirely on right needle.

This completes one knit stitch. Repeat Steps 1 through 4 in each stitch still on left needle. When the last stitch is worked, one row of knitting is completed.

Now measure your work. It should be about 7" wide. If it is too wide, start over and cast on fewer stitches; if it is too narrow, start over and cast on more stitches.

When the width is correct, begin next knit row as follows: turn right needle and hold it now in left hand. With free needle in right hand, work Steps 1 through 4 of First Knit Row in each stitch. Again take needle with stitches in left hand, and work another row of knit stitches. Work rows of knit stitches until block measures 9" long.

To complete the block, now bind off all the stitches.

Binding Off

Step 1: Knit the first 2 stitches; insert left needle into stitch you knitted first, and pull it over the second stitch and completely off the needle.

One stitch is now bound off.

Step 2: Knit one more stitch, insert left needle into first stitch on right needle, and pull it over the new stitch and completely off the needle. Another stitch is bound off; don't work too tightly.

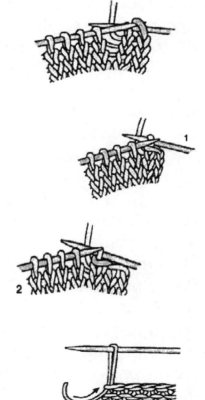

Repeat Step 2 until one stitch remains; now cut yarn from skein, leaving a 6" end. With needle draw end up and through last stitch to secure it. Thread yarn end into yarn needle and weave end into several stitches to secure it.

The first time you look at a crochet or knitting pattern, you'll probably think you're looking at a foreign language, because patterns traditionally are written using abbreviations. Most magazines or books will have a key explaining these abbreviations, but following is a helpful reference list.

Abbreviations:
approx…approximate(ly)
beg…begin(ning)
BLO…back loop only
BO…bind off
ch(s)…chain(s)
CC…contrasting color
CO…cast on
dc…double crochet
dec…decrease(ing)
DP or dpn…double pointed needle(s)
g or gr…grams
hdc…half double crochet
inc…increase(-ing)
in(s) or "…inch(es)
k…knit
k 2 tog…knit 2 stitches together
LH…left hand needle
lp(s)…loop(s)
MC…main color
M1…make one
oz…ounce(s)
patt(s)…pattern(s)
prev…previous
psso…pass slipped stitch over
p…purl
p-wise…purl-wise, or as though to purl

rem…remain(ing)
rep…repeat(ing)
RH…right hand needle
rnd(s)…round(s)
RS…right side
sc…single crochet
sk…skip
sl…slip
sl st(s)…slip stitches
sl 1, k 1, psso or SKP…slip 1 stitch as if to knit, knit 1 stitch, and pass the slipped stitch over the knit stitch, and over the end of the needle, or slip, knit, pass
sp(s)…space(s)
SP or spn…single-pointed needles
SSK…Slip, slip, knit. Slip first st as if to knit. Slip next st as if to knit. Put the tip of the left hand needle through the front of these two sts from left to right and knit them together.
st(s)…stitches(es)
St st…stockinette stitch

tog...together
tr...triple crochet(s)
WS...wrong side
YB or ytb...yarn to back of work
YF or ytf...yarn to front of work
yo...yarn over
YRN...yarn round needle

*...An asterisk is used to mark the beginning of a portion of instructions which will be worked more than once; thus, "rep between * * three times: means after working the instructions once, repeat the instructions between the asterisks 3 more times (4 times in all).

( )...Parentheses are used to enclose instructions which should be worked the exact number of times specified immediately following the parentheses, such as: (k1, p1) twice. They are also used to list the garment sizes and to provide additional information to clarify instructions.

[ ]...Brackets can be used in the same way as parentheses, but are usually used in combination with them to further clarify instructions.

SHORT & SWEET KNIT SCARF

They are all the rage: short, narrow scarves, that look great with a sweater or under a jacket. And you can make it quick with two strands of worsted-weight yarn. We used two variegated yarns to create these wonderful color combinations in our models but why not try combining a solid with a variegated yarn for a terrific tweedy look.

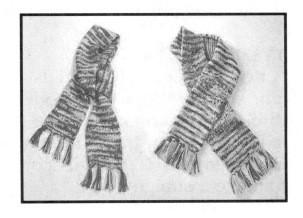

SIZE
One size fits all.

KNITTED MEASUREMENTS
5 1/2" by 56" (14 cm by 142.5 cm)

Materials:
Worsted-weight yarn (We used Caron International's Simply Soft yarn)
Size 8/H knitting needles
For blue/green scarf
1, 2.5 oz. skein of "Green Meadow"
1, 2.5 oz. skein of "Country Blue"

For maroon/purple scarf:
1, 2.5 oz. skein of "Sweet Violets"
1, 2.5 oz. skein of "Venetian Rose"

NOTE:
Hold 2 strands of yarn together throughout.

INSTRUCTIONS:
Cast on 25 stitches. Stockinette stitch (Knit all of the stitches in the first row. Purl all of the stitches in the second row.) Repeat, alternating knit and purl rows. for 280 rows, or until desire length. Bind off.

TASSELS:
For each tassel, cut 6 strands (3 of each colored yarn) into 8" (20.5 cm) strands. Hold them together and fold in half. Pull the yarn through the corner edge with a crochet needle inserted from back to front. Pull the strands through the loop. Repeat three times, spacing the tassels 1.25"/3cm apart. Repeat on other side. Trim tassels to make a straight edge.

For more information and help please contact:
Craft Yarn Council of America, 2500 Lowell Rd., Gastonia, NC 28054
Tel: 800-662-9999 •E-mail: cycainfo@aol.com •Fax: 704-824-0630
Websites:www.knitandcrochet.com • www.warmupamerica.com • www.learntoknit.com •
www.learntocrochet.com • www.teachknitting.com • www.teachcrochet.com • www.knit-out.com •
www.craftyarncouncil.com

You are now ready to place the finished objects that you have made into your hope chest! Your new hand-knitted, and crotcheted items are proof that you have the skills. Keep improving them. Don't quit now that you have just started. Try taking a bag of knitting or crotcheting with you when you are traveling a long way, when you are sitting in a group setting quietly, or when you are visiting in the evening.

You will also need to perfect your skills by the end of this book, for we will be making a baby layette!

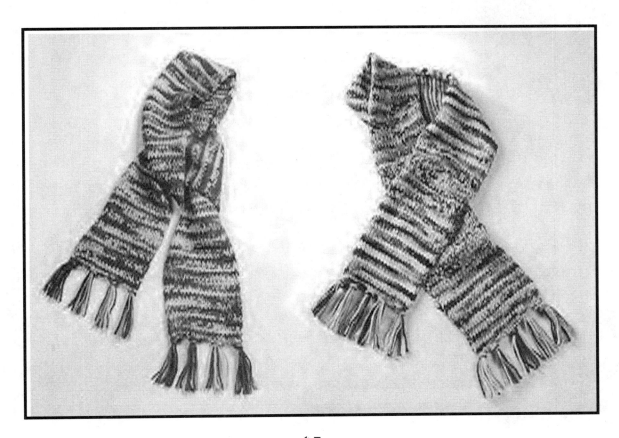

CHAPTER FIVE

✎ *Embroidery* ✎

"She layeth her hands to the spindle,
and her hands hold the distaff."
Proverbs 3:19

Every hope chest was not complete until the young lady knew how to embroider a sampler perfectly. This was to show that all of the knowledge of the finer art of embroidery had been accomplished.

The uses for embroidery are endless. You may embroider pillowcases, tea towels, little girl's dresses, handkerchiefs, linens and more!

The ancient art of embroidery is a skill you will thoroughly enjoy. All you need to know are a few simple embroidery stitches using a needle and thread, and you are on your way to making beautiful items for your home. You should try all these basic stitches on a scrap piece of fabric. Then you will make a sampler following. Try to find a dark linen scrap and then use white or golden yellow embroidery thread. You need to draw a pattern with white fabric chalk.

Do not get discouraged if at first you find needlework a bit awkward. Soon you will be sewing away, making the most beautiful handicraft that you will lovingly display in your own home someday.

Take your time and enjoy the peace that comes with quiet hand work!

We would like to thank the Craft Yarn Council of America who helped us with the following projects. For more information and help you can go to their web page at: www.learntoknit.com

Step by Step Decorative Embroidery Stitches

1. *Outline or Stem Stitch* — You work this stitch from left to right. Bring the needle up through the fabric to right side on the drawn line to be outlined. Hold the thread toward you and take a short slanting back stitch along your line on the fabric. Stitch from right to left and bring the needle out to the left at the end of previous stitch. Repeat along your pattern, and make sure to keep your stitches small and uniform.

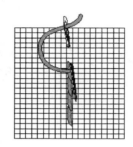

2. *Whipped Stem Stitch* — This is to outline your design in one color; then, in a different color of thread, whipstitch over the stem stitch.

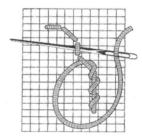

3. *Running Stitch*—You use this stitch for outlining and padding. You make small up and down stitches by carrying the needle in and out of the material. Take several stitches on needle before drawing through.

4. *Whipped Running Stitch* — With a running stitch, outline the design. Now whip stitch over running stitch.

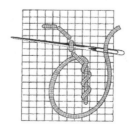

When you stitch, make sure that you start by going through the wrong side of the material. Don't ever make a knot. You make two or three small stitches in the same place to anchor the thread.

5. *Chain Stitch*—Bring the thread to right side of your material, then hold the thread toward you with your left thumb. Next, take a stitch into the same hole where the thread was brought up, it will form a small loop. Loosely, bring your needle out a short distance forward and over the loop. Overlap the first loop and make a second one. Continue along your pattern.

6. *Back Stitch*— Stitch a small running stitch, then insert the needle at the end of the running stitch, pierce needle through to the wrong side and over twice as much space as the first stitch on wrong side. Bring the needle over to right side and repeat it again.

7. *Herringbone Stitch*—This stitch looks like two rows of backstitch on the right side. On the wrong side, the catch stitch. It is for see-through material because the threads that cross will show through to the right side. Slant the needle the same as if you are making a catch stitch, then make a single back stitch, first on the lower side and then diagonally across on the upper side. When the crosses are worked on the right side it is called the herringbone stitch.

8. *Daisy Stitch*---Bring the needle up at the center point of the petal, hold the thread towards you. Thrust the needle down at inner point of the petal, 1 or 2 threads to the right of the point where thread comes out. Bring the tip of the needle out at outer end of petal, going over the thread. Draw a loop up to cover petal, pierce needle down outside of the loop to fasten it in place. Bring the needle out at inner point of next petal to left or right.

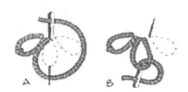

9. *Cross Stitch*--- Try to make a design first on checked gingham or a weave like monk's cloth. Make a slanting stitch from the lower left hand corner of square to the upper right corner of the square. Make a second slanting stitch from lower right of the same square to the upper left corner of cross. All crosses should be worked the same way so that they are all alike. If you have a long row to make, you can go all across the same way and then back crossing all the stitches in the other direction.

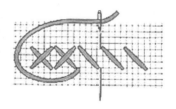

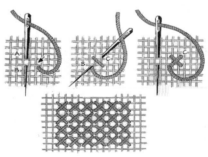

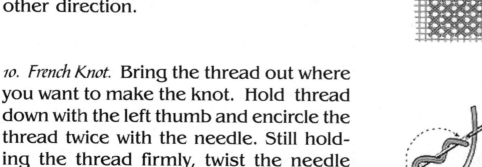

10. *French Knot.* Bring the thread out where you want to make the knot. Hold thread down with the left thumb and encircle the thread twice with the needle. Still holding the thread firmly, twist the needle back to the starting point and insert it close to where the thread first emerged .

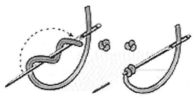

Pull thread through to the back and secure for a single french knot or pass on to the position of the next stitch.

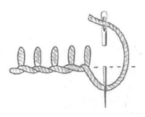

11. *Blanket Stitch*---Bring the thread out on the lower line, insert the needle in position in the upper line, taking a straight downward stitch with the thread under the needle- point. Pull up the stitch to form a loop and repeat.

12. *Feather Stitch*---Fig. A - bring the needle out at the top centre, hold the thread down with the left thumb, insert the needle a little to the right on the same level and take a small stitch down to the centre, keeping the thread under the needle point. Next, insert the needle a little to the left on the same level and take a stitch to the center, keeping the thread under the needle point. Work these two movements alternately.
Fig. B - shows Double Feather Stitch, in which two stitches are taken to the right and left alternately.

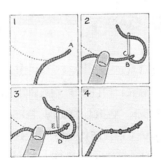

13. *Couching Stitch*---Hold a heavy thread or cord or several threads along the line to be followed. Bring needle, threaded with finer thread, up close to cord. Thrust needle down on opposite side of cord to make a stitch at right angles to it. Bring needle up

to left in position for another right angle stitch. Continue taking stitches over cord, spacing them evenly.

Interesting effects of the couching stitch may be achieved by working over several threads in the blanket stitch, the chain stitch and the feather stitch.

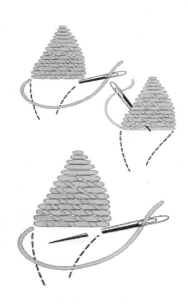

14. Bokhara Couching Stitch---The thread to be couched is laid across the space from left to right; using the same thread fasten down with small slanting stitches at even intervals.

After you have learned to make each of these stitches and have become captivated with the idea of embroidery, you will want to make something useful and pretty right away. There is a wonderful selection on the market which will help you make items that you could never ever hope to buy. Try embroidering with beautiful threads such as nylon or shining rayon threads, shiny cotton, embroidery floss, or even metallic thread! Contrasting color gives an bright and happy effect. Try embroidering with yarn on jackets, belts, fabric purses and more. You can embroider guest towels, pillow slips, aprons, washcloths, luncheon sets and many other gift ideas, to personalize and enhance your gifts!

Handkerchief Embroidery

You will love to create these old-fashioned handkerchiefs. You can purchase handkerchiefs at JC Penneys and other department stores. If they do not carry any in your area, you may also find men's white handkerchiefs and dye them any color you wish. You simply take a pencil and lightly draw a design on the fabric. Next you simply embroider using any of the previous stitches.

What you need:

~Handkerchief
~Embroidery floss
~Embroidery needle
~Small embroidery hoop

1. Lightly draw on your design.

2. Place your cloth tightly in your embroidery hoop.

3. Embroidery your design, choosing to use any previous stitches.

(If you feel really daring, you may wish to crochet around the edges with a fine hook and thread.)

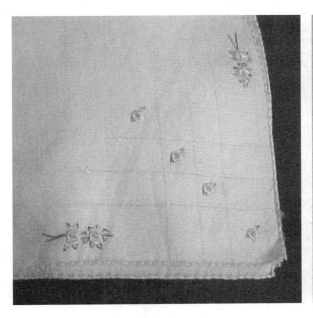 

The following pattern should be traced onto a rectangular piece of light fabric. You may use fabric copy paper and a tracer found in the sewing section of your store.

Xerox this pattern for an embroidery sampler.

CHAPTER SIX

Sewing

"He that sews bountifully,
shall reap bountifully..."
2 Corinthians 9:6
(It says sowest, really.)

Sewing is a very challenging and satisfying art. Did you know Adam and Eve were the first ones on earth to sew? In Genesis 3:7 it tells us that "And the eyes of them both were opened, and they knew that they were naked; and they sewed fig leaves together, and made themselves aprons."

Sadly, this was because they had disobeyed God, and would have never known their nakedness if they would not have eaten of the tree of the knowledge of good and evil.

God must not have liked their sewing job, because it says later in vs. 21, "Unto Adam also and to his wife did the Lord God make coats of skins, and clothed them."

Needless to say, sewing has been around since the very beginning of mankind. Ever since we've had the need to sew clothing after the fall, people have been sewing away.

It is very difficult in our day and age to find clothing that is really feminine and pretty. Most of the clothing that you will find in department stores are very uni-sex. Some stores do not even carry dresses. The only thing they stock are pants and shirts, even in the girl's department. When you do find those rare dresses, they cost an arm and a leg!

This is where sewing becomes essential to the preparation of the future homemaker.

Let's start with the very beginning information you will need. Take your beautiful new sewing basket that you have made, and let's begin by stocking it with necessary sewing equipment...

Stocking Your Sewing Basket

The following items you can purchase from an inexpensive dime store like Walgreens, K-mart, WalMart or even your Dollar store.

Scissors
Pins
Pincushion
Tape measure
Needles
Thimble
White & Black thread
Seam Ripper

1. *Scissors* - Over the years, we have found that the best scissors that are gentle on little and big hands, are the ones with the springs.

To the right is a picture of our favorite. Scissors are used for cutting material, cutting out your patterns, cutting thread, and more! (Hint: Never use your material scissors on paper.)

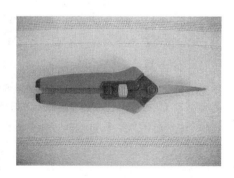

2. *Pincushion* - This is another important item. You need to have these in order to keep your home safe from pins on the floor. Always keep it close by when sewing.

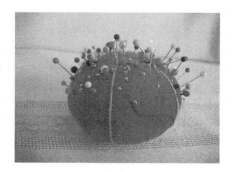

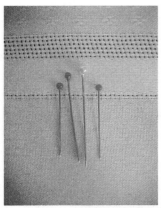

3. *Pins* - Do not use the thick, steel head pins. They do not go through the fabric well, and will cause you a lot of frustration.

Purchase the long, skinny needles with the colored balls on top. They are easy to use, and also easy to find when they drop!

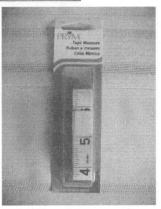

4. *Measuring Tape* - You will need this to measure length. We have used ours to measure our waists, our length for making a hem, and more. You also use it for making blocks, which we will be doing further on in this chapter.

5. *Needles* - In large sewing stores they have packets of all different sizes of needles. Some people like their needles longer than others. To begin with, use the longer needles with the larger eye holes. This will make them easier to thread.

6. *Thimble* - You will need this when you are hand stitching in order to not piece your thumb. Purchase only the inexpensive type with the indented, tiny, bumps surrounding the top. There are thimbles which are much more expensive, but they are useless because they don't have those indents.

7. *White & Black thread* - Always have a light and dark thread on hand in order to mend rips.

8. *Seam Ripper* - These are invaluable when sewing with a sewing machine. Whenever you make a mistake and sew along the wrong place, you simply take out your ripper and take out the thread.

There are many more tools which will help you with your sewing, but these are just the basics which you will need for your next project...

Making a Hand Sewn Baby Quilt

This is a project that every young girl will enjoy. You will learn the simple art of sewing by hand and create a lovely baby quilt that you will want to place in your hope chest. Take your time, enjoy each stitch, and savor the sweet peace that comes with sewing!

What you will need:

~ 3 1/2 yards of light material
~ 2 yards of contrasting darker material
~ 2 yards of quilting batting
~ Thread to match the contrasting material
~ Yarn (matching)

The idea is to make a checker board using small square pieces of material.

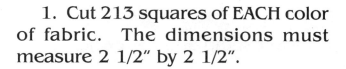

Pattern of
Actual size

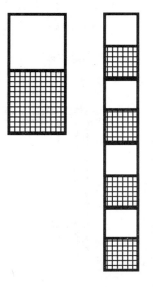

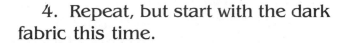

1. Cut 213 squares of EACH color of fabric. The dimensions must measure 2 1/2" by 2 1/2".

2. The easiest way to do this is to have your mother help you to fold the fabric so that you will cut 10 pieces at one time.

3. Starting with the light fabric, sew contrasting squares together and make a long row, 25 squares in length. Remember to sew on the WRONG side of the material.

(The wrong side of the material is the unfinished side that doesn't show the design as well as the front. The RIGHT side of the material is the finished side which shows the design.)

4. Repeat, but start with the dark fabric this time.

5. Sew together the two rows of 25 squares, making sure that the colors are checkered (every other one).

6. Repeat steps 3-5 until you have 17 rows of the 25 length rows sown together. **Iron** your quilt. Pressing seams outward.

The batting and the back:

7. Measure your finished quilted project.

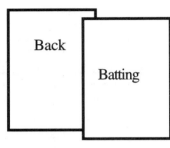

8. Cut from the lighter material, the same size of fabric as the quilted front.

9. Next, using the same dimensions, cut a piece of batting.

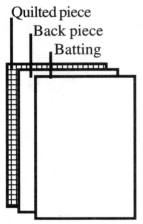

10. On the ground, lay the quilted piece, RIGHT side up.

11. Next, lay the back piece WRONG side UP (the two right sides are facing) on top of the quilted piece.

12. On top, lay the batting.

13. You are going to sew all around the edge leaving a 6" space NOT SEWN. (You may ask your mother to machine sew this, if you would like). Sew 1/4" in from the edge, all the way around the blanket.

14. Next, turn your blanket inside out. You will see it start looking like a real baby blanket!

15. Sew the 6" turn space together and finish.

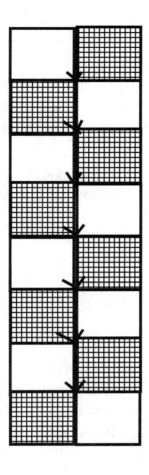

16. Finish with Yarn. You are going to sew little knots of yarn at the intersection of all the squares on your quilt.

You thread a yarn needle with a long piece of yarn. The quilted side of your blanket and thrust through to the bottom side. Don't pull through, just go about 1/8 of an inch through all layers and come up to the top again. Cut your yarn leaving at least an inch of yarn in order to tie a knot.

You are doing this to stabilize your batting. If you didn't do this, when you wash your blanket the batting would become lumpy and unpleasant for a baby to snuggle.

17. Cutting the yarn. In order for the quilt to look nice, take some small scissors and cut the ends of the yarn so that they are all the same length. Some people only leave little ends, others like to have them 1/4 or 1/2 inch long. It depends on what you like. Just keep them uniform (the same length).

When you have finished, place this item in your hope chest to show that you have completed the skill of sewing by hand!

The Sewing Machine

When starting to use a sewing machine, it is so important that you are supervised by your mother. Sit down together and have her explain to you how the sewing machine functions.

Learn to thread the machine, to operate the foot pedal, to go forward and backward, to go slow and fast, and to knot the beginning and end of a stitch.

You may wish to tackle the baby blanket, only when you start, this time use the sewing machine.

Keep your stitches very straight. Do not try to go too fast with the machine.

At the end of this book you will find a reference chapter for all of the chapters (clubs) of The American Sewing Guild. This Guild is a wonderful place to find older women who are experts in sewing. They also are hoping to help keep the art of sewing continuing into future generations and happily welcome new young ladies into their groups.

They are located throughout each state and each group typically covers an area ranging from 50 to 75 miles. Some have Neighborhood Groups which meet at various times to help the needs of local members.

If you want information about a specific location and its Neighborhood group, go to these pages and they will help you. If you find that there is not one in your area, you can contact the Association headquarters directly for guidelines on starting your own Chapter of ASG.

We pray that you are excited with your newly acquired skills! Remember to start simple and then work your way up to tackling new sewing challenges at different levels. You will soon be able to tackle, well, maybe a wedding dress! ... Soon...

Now, add your blanket to your hope chest!

Here is a stenciled border in a living room.
Decorate any room with stencils.

CHAPTER SEVEN

Decorating

"Every wise woman buildeth her house; but the foolish plucketh it down with her hands."
Proverbs 14:1

Decorating your room and home shouldn't be something very difficult for you to learn. It can all be summed up in one three word sentence...

Keep it simple.

Many times people try to gather many objects and try to place them all over their home. Most of the time, it will not be in good taste! One way to keep your room from becoming too cluttered is to keep all your items that you just can't part with inside a bookshelf with glass doors.

The ones pictured on the previous page were purchased at K-Mart for under $60 on sale. This is where they have kept heirlooms and other items that they wished to keep away from tiny hands.

What happens when you do not keep it simple is that you will find your house becoming the following:

-Cluttered & messy.
-Actually dirty, as dust will accumulate on objects & if not properly dusted, will become solid dirt.
-Unorganized, as you will never be able to find what you need

amidst your clutter.

-Health hazard, as you will start developing allergies, and also, if you are one who places things on the floor, you could break a leg.

Another way of being simple is to not purchase expensive items. Purchasing expensive items in a home that trains children is simply asking for disappointment and disaster.

I knew of a woman who had nine children and bought a very expensive dining table for them to eat at. It was the sort of table that would belong in a mansion on a hill. It would have to be polished after every formal meal eaten there.

After one week this fancy table looked like the old one they had replaced seven days ago. Scratch marks, table burns from hot drinks being placed on the wood, permanent markers, had quickly brought the table to match the shape of its predecessor.

Right now, dear sister, give up *lady of the manor* thoughts and decide to live within the means that your future husband can provide. Do not store up fancy treasures here on earth. Women who store up expensive treasures in their homes do not make it a place where children can be trained properly. They are too worried about the children breaking their material possessions, or are focused only on adding to their earthly collection.

Remember this scripture:

"Do not lay up for yourselves treasures on earth, where moth and rust destroy and where thieves break in and steal, but lay up for yourselves treasures in heaven, where neither moth nor rust destroys and where thieves do not break in and steal." Matthew 6:19-21

You don't have to have expensive items in your home to make it beautiful. There are many wise, God-fearing women, whose husband do not make much money. In fact, according to the world's standards they are labeled "poor"! But these clever women who are walking in God's wisdom are not poor in their eyes, nor in their Heavenly Father's eyes for they have learned something that the world doesn't know. They have learned to be frugal! This means that they can make a penny go as far, or further, than a dollar!

One of the most important accomplishments that you should strive for is learning to use what you have on hand and to be creative.

There are women whose husbands have purchased inexpensive, fix-er-up homes. When they have first seen the homes they may have shuddered with horror. Chipped paint, broken hinges, dirty carpet, filthy walls, weedy yard, no grass, may have made even the bravest of women gulp. But with a little common sense and wisdom from God, that dilapidated house can be turned into the most lovely and beautiful home!

When you are first married, you probably will only be able to afford a small home which may need a lot of care. With just a little amount of money, but with lots of creative ideas and elbow grease, you can turn trash into treasure!

The following projects will help to give you some ideas and training in home decorating for your future.

The first we will be working on is stenciling. We chose stenciling over all other forms of home decorating because it is the least expensive, it is the easiest, and the one that is less complicated in the end to change if you don't like it!

Unlike wallpapering, which is expensive to buy, hard to remove and almost impossible to easily change if you don't like it, stenciling can be done by those who don't believe they have any talent in art or decorating.

The following stencil designs and how to's have been provided by The Stencil Shoppe. For over 1200 designs, please write or call for a catalogue:

The Stencil Shoppe, Inc.
2503 Silverside Road
Wilmington, DE 19810
Phone: 302-475-7975
Toll Free: 1-800-822-STEN (7836)

Let's start with a project and just use a long piece of fabric to practice stenciling on. Use 2 yards of white cotton fabric, ironed. First, you must choose a stencil. Next, you must purchase the following inexpensive supplies...

Stencil Supplies

Brushes - We suggest a stencil brush for each color used.

Large (1 1/4", 1", 3/4") brush for large openings
Medium (5/8", 1/2") for medium openings (flowers or narrow vines)
Small (3/8", 1/4") for tiny openings or when one color is close to another.

Paint - You may use waterbased paint in 2 oz. bottles. One bottle per color will be enough for a normal sized room. Two bottles will be necessary if one color is predominant. If you prefer oil based paint, stencil paintsticks or small tubs are available.

Miscellaneous - masking tape, spray adhesive (helps hold large stencils) paper or styrofoam plates, paper towels, a level for placing stencils in a mural or when you need a straight line, a permanent pen for additional regular marks.

How to Stencil and shading ideas

STEP 1
Position the stencil with part #1 of the stencil in the left corner of your wall. Use masking tape or spray adhesive to hold the stencil to the surface. Pour out a small amount of paint (size of a quarter) on your plate. Dip your brush into the paint you want to use first.

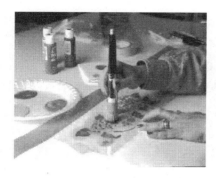

STEP 2

Dab the brush on a paper towel to remove excess paint. Swirl the brush in a circular motion, working the paint into the bristles. Less paint is better ... you can always apply more. If you dab the brush on the back of your hand and no paint rubs off - you are ready to proceed.

STEP 3

Apply the paint to the stencil openings in either a circular (swirling) or a tapping (pouncing) motion. (See backside for details). Move from the outside to the middle of the opening.

STEP 4

Line up additional overlays using the black drawn register marks. The markings will lay overtop a previously stenciled section of the design ensuring proper alignment of the design. Continue stenciling with additional colors.

STEP 5

Remove the Overlay to see the full effect. The design should have clean, crisp edges. Too much paint will appear blotchy and bleed underneath the stencil. If this happens, make sure to wipe the stencil dry before continuing.

STEP 6

Repeat the design by lining up the left hand register mark on part # 1 with the right section of the design on the wall. When

These stencils are available from The Stencil Shoppe, 1-800-822-7836

you come to a corner, try to end with the whole of the design (i.e. fudge a little to finish your design so that half of a leaf, apple, house, etc. will be divided on each wall.)

Wash the stencil periodically, preferably every thirty minutes. This prevents clogging of the openings and drying of paint on the stencil. Use cool to warm water and soap, wiping carefully towards the center of the cutout so as not to tear any bridges. Some very intricate stencils are difficult to clean, so be very careful or just wipe excess paint off. Murphy's Oil Soap is recommended.

You will love the different effects you can acquire with stenciling!

Try stenciling the following:

~Old furniture

~Lampshades

~Windowsill

~Waste paper baskets

~Curtains

These stencils are available from The Stencil Shoppe.

These stencils are available from The Stencil Shoppe, 1-800-822-7836

The ideas are limitless! You can create the most beautiful rooms with just three little bottles of paint and matching brushes. Plan now for your favorite patterns which you will have in your home. Practice on your own room in order to perfect your skill.

If you get really good, I bet your mother will even want you to do more rooms in the house!

Place your stencils which you are collecting in the bottom of your hope chest in an envelope.

You now have completed another helpful skill for your future days of being a homemaker!

These stencils are available from The Stencil Shoppe.

Picture Frames

One of the easiest ways of decorating simply is to use pictures to make your rooms prettier!

You can use prints that you buy at the art or hobby store, or you can do what many people are finding the most economical way of finding prints... use cards! There are so many greeting cards to choose from that sometimes it is hard to make a decision!

Depending on the room that you are wanting to decorate, keep in mind the main color scheme, and the item that you are going to frame.

For example, in our daughter's room we have antique dolls, an antique phone we found at a garage sale and she also loves flowers. The greeting cards we chose to frame contained dolls and flowers!

In our bathroom we have chosen cards which have scriptures on them. They are the same basic colors that our stenciling is.

When choosing, it is very important to keep the color in mind.

The whole process of framing greeting cards is so very simple and inexpensive; but, can, amazingly, brighten any room!

What you will need:

~A favorite greeting card, chosen with the room you would like to decorate in mind.

~A picture frame that is the same size as the card.

~Wall nails & hammer.

~Ribbon, matching - a yard long.

~Glue.

1. Take the photo of your choice and make sure that all of the edges are even. There is nothing more distressful than a picture that is placed crooked in a frame! No matter how often you straighten the frame on the wall, it can never be corrected!

2. Next, open the back of your frame and prepare the glass for your photo. Make sure that the glass has no fingerprints on the inside, as they will be there permanently.

3. Cut four small pieces of tape, masking tape or invisible work great, and secure the photo in straight. Replace the back.

4. Next, cut some ribbon that matches your decorating scheme of the room that your picture is going into, about 1 yard long. Take 12 inches and make a pretty bow.

5. Now take the remaining ribbon and with a small nail, hang it straight down the wall. Glue your ribbon at the top. Hang your picture in the middle of the length of ribbon. Voila! You have a beautiful wall decoration!
(See picture at left.)

Another decorating idea that some people like to use is that of seasonal decorations. We have family decorations for each of the seasons. Flowers for spring and summer (we just change which flowers); fall items such as leaves, pilgrims, & squash; and snowmen for winter! Our furniture is bare when we don't have our seasonal items out; but, bring them out and it turns the house into a fun home for the children to enjoy!

Decorating your home comes from your heart. If you don't feel creative, ask the Lord and He will show you ideas! Remember that the most important thing is to keep it simple. Don't clutter or feel that every space must have an item to show.

Try not to be a pack rat and keep every material item that you find. Have a generous heart and give away those things which you will not use in your life!

Make gifts of your favorite greeting card frames and give them for any special occasion. They are something that you can give in love from your heart, and know that anyone would be happy to have such a gift!

Your skills are accumulating! Keep returning to the previous ones that you have learned and perfect each one.

Now that you have learned to frame pictures, to stencil your walls, the rest is up to your imagination! Place one finished framed picture that you hope to hang in your home one day, along with any stencils that you have chosen, in your hope chest.

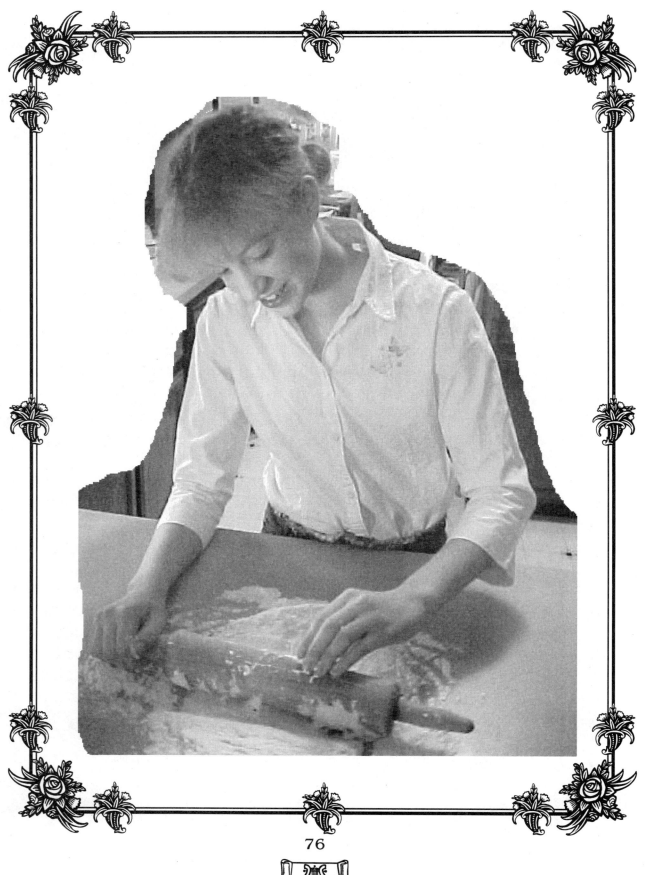

CHAPTER EIGHT

⌇ *Kitchen Preparation* ⌇

"She is like the merchant ships;
she brings her food from afar."
Proverbs 31:14

This chapter is going to be devoted to one of the most important aspects of preparation for marriage. Feeding your loved ones... You are going to find that one of the places that you will be spending a lot of time is in your kitchen.

Every young lady needs to start planning and learning about the utensils and items that she will need for her own kitchen. Without the proper tools and knowledge regarding kitchen items, you will not be armed with what you will need to raise a healthy and happy family!

Many of these items you will want to start collecting; but, do not put them in your hope chest. Store them in clean boxes in your garage, attic or storage shed.

Do keep inventory of what you are collecting and keep a list in your hope chest of what you do have and what you need.

Many items will be given to you before you get married at a wedding shower, and then later as wedding presents. But remember, many people today do not think practically regarding needs of newlyweds, because they assume the woman will not be a homemaker. There are plenty of statues and whatnots lining the shelves of Goodwill Stores which have been given as wedding presents. Do not depend on your marriage gifts, but plan ahead.

Again, garage sales are a wonderful place to find all the items that you will need!

Use the following list and check off each item after you have obtained them.

Check List for Kitchen Preparation:

Pots & Pans
(Use stainless steel or Pyrex glass for health's sake.)

- ☐ One oblong cake sheet
- ☐ Two pie pans
- ☐ Two round cake tins
- ☐ One large cookie sheet
- ☐ One large skillet w/lid
- ☐ One medium skillet
- ☐ One small skillet
- ☐ One pancake skillet (no edges)
- ☐ One 12-count muffin pan
- ☐ Colander (strainer)
- ☐ Large baking casserole dish with lid (pyrex)

Utensils

- ☐ 8 Knives
- ☐ 8 Forks
- ☐ 8 Spoons
- ☐ 8 Soup spoons
- ☐ 8 Steak knives
- ☐ 8 Salad forks
- ☐ 8 Butter knives
- ☐ 4 Large serving spoons
- ☐ Salad serving set
- ☐ 1 Large slicing knife
- ☐ 2 Sharp paring knives
- ☐ 4 Strainer serving spoons
(they have holes in the spoon)

- ☐ One bread knife
- ☐ Spatula
- ☐ Ladle for serving soup
- ☐ Rolling pin
- ☐ Four wooden spoons
- ☐ Kitchen scissors

Kitchen Mixing Bowls

- ☐ 3-piece set of mixing bowls with lids, (plastic)
- ☐ 3-piece set of mixing bowls with lids, (metal)
- ☐ Small leftover containers with lids. Tupperware has some great ones!

Plates & Dishes

- ☐ 8 Dinner plates
- ☐ 8 Salad plates
- ☐ 8 Bread plates
- ☐ 8 Soup bowls
- ☐ 8 Fruit bowls
- ☐ 8 Coffee plates
- ☐ 8 Coffee cups
- ☐ 2 Serving plates
- ☐ 2 Large serving bowls

Kitchen Equipment

- ☐ Electric hand mixer
- ☐ Carrot/Potato peeler
- ☐ Can opener
- ☐ Bottle opener
- ☐ Measuring Spoons
- ☐ Measuring Cups
- ☐ Flour sifter
- ☐ Whisk (for gravy)
- ☐ Food processor ($20 from Walmart or Sams)
- ☐ Cheese/carrot grater
- ☐ Blender
- ☐ Toaster
- ☐ Waffle Iron

Kitchen Linens

- ☐ 8 Hand towels
- ☐ 8 Dishcloths
- ☐ 2 Hot mitts
- ☐ 2 Tablecloths
- ☐ 8 Cloth napkins
- ☐ 8 Hot pads to place hot dishes upon
- ☐ 8 Place mats
- ☐ Kitchen aprons

Kitchen Wish List

- ☐ Wheat Grinder
- ☐ Bread Machine
- ☐ Large Mixer
- ☐ Juicer
- ☐ Ice cream machine

When obtaining the previous list, remember the following:
(We will explain why further on in the chapter.)

~ *Do not purchase items made from aluminum.*

~ *Do not buy expensive china items or serving dishes.*

~ *Stay away from crystal or anything else with lead in the glass.*

~ *Buy cotton products. They pick up dirt better and also are easier to clorox.*

~ *Look for your better made kitchen equipment which will last throughout your lifetime, and then your children's also. They may cost a bit more up front, but that is better than having to buy a new one every five years!*

- ☐ _____
- ☐ _____
- ☐ _____
- ☐ _____
- ☐ _____
- ☐ _____
- ☐ _____
- ☐ _____

The previous list was, hopefully, all the basic items that you will need when you take up housekeeping! There will be more that you will accumulate, such as cookie guns, coffee machines, I'm sure that your mother probably has some extras; but, they are not necessary when you first begin.

Over the years, mothers have found certain health helps regarding the use of metals.

ALUMINUM POISONING

Why it is dangerous to buy aluminum pans & kitchen utensils.—After use of these products, doctors have come to believe that aluminum poisoning causes symptoms which are similar to those of Alzheimer's Disease and osteoporosis.

Other symptoms which may occur include gastrointestinal problems, colic, rickets, extreme nervousness, headache, anemia, poor kidney and liver function, speech disturbances, memory loss, weak and aching muscles, and softening of bones.

Many doctors now believe that Alzheimer's disease is caused by aluminum poisoning.

Aluminum was not commonly used until the 1940's when an inexpensive method was found to extract it from Bauxite by running an electric current through the ore. Physicians now believe that there is a direct relationship from the heavy increase of Alzheimer's Disease to that of aluminum use.

Why is it so poisonous to the human system? Aluminum hinders the body in absorbing calcium and other minerals. It has been firmly proven that aluminum salts in the brain reduces our mental abilities and causes seizures. When patients having Alzheimer's Disease have died, they have studied their brains to find that they have four times the amount of aluminum compared with others who did not have the disease.

Not only does aluminum hurt the brain, it also damages the kidneys which try to excrete it from the body.

Where do we have to be careful when avoiding aluminum poisoning?—Aluminum pots, pans, and other cookware. Aluminum foil, antiperspirants, deodorants, bleached flour, regular table salt, tobacco smoke, processed cheese, cream of tartar, douches, canned goods, baking powder, antacids, buffered aspirin, and most city water. Processed cheese is high in it, for the aluminum helps it melt when heated.

This is why we tell our daughters to never use aluminum cookware! Use stainless steel or glass whenever possible.

LEAD POISONING

Why should we avoid lead crystal and other products which contain lead?—Lead poisoning causes children and adults to not be able to control their behavior.

So often as we gaze at the magazine tabloids or fancy homemaking magazine which is advertising the latest elegantly set table, we see beautiful crystal goblets gracing the decor.

Don't fall into this trap! Even though many of the manufacturers of lead crystal say that it is absolutely harmless to drink from, don't believe it.

Chronic lead poisoning causes reproductive disorders, even to the point where you may not even be able to have children because of prolonged exposure! Many doctors now believe that there is a relationship to sudden infant death syndrome when infants are exposed to high lead levels than those who die of other causes.

Continuing to use lead products result in damage to the liver, kidneys, heart, and nervous system. Some symptoms of those suffering from lead poisoning is that they will have days of severe gastrointestinal colic. Their gums turn blue and they have muscle weakness. Paralysis of the extremities, blindness, mental disturbances, protein disorder, loss of memory, mental retardation, and even insanity can eventually result.

Where do you find lead besides in crystal? —Lead is extremely toxic, and it is found in leaded gasoline; lead pipes; and other piping using solder, ceramic glazes, lead-based paints, and lead-acid batteries. Lead arsenate is an insecticide used on certain plants. Another reason why mother's milk is so much better for little babies is that lead is in commercial baby milk!

People also consume lead when they use tobacco, eat liver, and drink domestic or imported wines. Lead is also used in the production of some soda pop cans.

What must you do for your future family?—Always read your labels. (Although pop cans do not mention the ingredients in the metal of the can!)

Buy only canned goods which are lead-free. These cans have been welded and have no soldered side seems. Do not use imported canned goods; no regulations cover them.

Avoid breathing the air too often near a highway. Car exhausts contribute to terrible lead fumes and other harmful chemicals which are in the smoke. Imagine what happens when you grow a garden near a highway!

When you have the opportunity to purchase your first home, try not to buy one that is built before 1986. Lead pipes and soldering was not banned until this year and many people are slowly being poisoned in homes which have these without even knowing it!

Watch drinking out of hand made pottery or cups which are imported. The glaze has lead and many studies have been done which have shown that foreign countries do not regulate the lead in this glaze.

The China Syndrome

Unfortunately, many young people make the mistake of purchasing good china. Unless you find it at a garage sale, or unless you are gifted by your grandmother or another relative, do not put your money into this expensive, but fragile, temptation.

One thing that causes a young woman to not be satisfied with her lot in life is when she tries to keep up with the glamour of the Jones's. Realize here and now that a beautiful, bouncing baby that cries, burps, spits and poo's is worth a millions times more than a piece of fragile glass that, if used or touched wrong, shatters into a million pieces.

There is not much wisdom in purchasing items that can't be used with children. Can a child eat on china? No. Can a child drink out of heavy crystal? No. By pursuing these worthless treasures and protecting them from our children we

are following the folly of the world! Rather, as Christians, we should do it the other way around. We need to protect our children and shun the worthless treasures that are just temporary.

There is nothing evil in having a beautiful china set. Just be ready to have that china set broken if you use it daily with children!

How much more sense is there in having dishes and glasses and utensils which are child safe and where there are no tears shed when they finally do go to the garbage pail in the sky!

I think that young ladies who are always looking around at what other people may have, will find that they will not be able to be as content as those who do not eyeball material objects of others. The Bible tells us in the tenth commandment that "we are not to covet anything that our neighbor has". Coveting means to look at what others have and then want it. This is also what people do who are always trying to keep up with the material objects of the Jones's.

There are many homes where children are abundant and the

women of the home can still set a beautiful table.

There are absolutely beautiful designs painted on the most delicate glass, but they are not expensive and they are easy to replace. Corningware is our favorite place to find place settings and you can get a complete service of 8 (8 dinner plates, 8 bowls, 8 salad plates, etc.) for under $30!

Many young ladies have also found matching place settings at garage sales, including the silverware, all for under $10. People get new dishes, and think nothing of selling a $400 piece set of silverware for $5 or $10, simply to get it out of the house!

Take advantage of your local flea market and garage sales. They are ran by people like you and I, those who are trying to get rid of those things they do not need.

You can also check your Goodwill Store or Salvation Army Thrift Store for all the items on this list.

One thing to be cautious of is whether the metal objects contain aluminum or not. Another thing to watch for is the thinness of the metal. Aluminum is very thin and bends and dents easily.

Finding Your Linens

Many daughters have made the majority of their linens. They have purchased the light cotton canvas squares for kitchen towels and have embroidered delightful flowers or other designs on them.

Kitchen towels can be found for very little money at McFrugal type stores for under a dollar. TJ Maxx also carries them in their clearance aisle sometimes. We have purchased some for under 50 cents!

We have also purchased fine linen tablescloths and napkins there for under $5! Look in the clearance section after each season ends.

The following hot pad designs were purchased from Walmart in their craft section. You can vary the colors if you wish. The designs are beautiful and decorate an area all by themselves!

Before you close this chapter, make sure that you sit with your mother and show her the list that is at the beginning. She may have some extra items to give you. Do this with her! She will be delighted to help you on your way towards having a kitchen of your own some day.

Copy the list, place it in your hope chest, and as you obtain all necessary items, check them off. Keep the items in labeled boxes and write that label next to your item on your check list. This will help you remember where they are in the future.

CHAPTER NINE

∽ *Cooking* ∾

"Give us this day our daily bread."
Matthew 6:11

As a mother or young lady, you will find that you spend a majority of your time in the kitchen. Besides just cooking food, you are going to be responsible for keeping your family in good health by feeding them the nutrition that they need.

I know that sometimes studying the affects of vitamins and minerals may sound overwhelming, but you need to know this for health's sake.

The following information will give you the pros and cons of vitamins and what happens with too much or too little.

Your family's health will literally be in your hands (Regarding food, of course. Our very lives and our wellness being first in God's hands!) when it comes to what you are allowing to go into their systems.

We all know people who are not temperate with their concern of food items and go over board in their attempt at making sure they eat healthy. You do not want to be obsessed with food either in a lusty, gluttonous sense, nor do you want to be obsessed with it in a over-virtuous sense of eating right. Those who are so obsessed will even get to the point of making a fuss when invited over to someone's house for dinner, if they didn't fix what they considered "good for them".

Studying Good Nutrition

Protein is very easily obtainable from plant products. Too much protein causes calcium to be leached from the bones, and too little causes vitamin deficiencies. How much do you need? You should be eating 1 gram of protein per day for every 2.2 pounds of your body weight.

Calcium is very important for strong, healthy bones. But contrary to popular belief, the best way to obtain it is not from milk, but from plants. Some calcium rich foods include: tofu, soy milk, fortified orange juice, broccoli, sesame seeds, navy beans, raisins, kidney beans, almonds, among others.

Iron is a concern for many young ladies as they enter into womanhood, so you must make sure that you eat enough foods with iron. Great sources of iron include: meat, bran flakes, tofu, chickpeas, pumpkin seeds, apricots, and raisins. Vitamin C helps aide the absorption of Iron, so drink plenty of orange juice.

Vitamin D is normally found in animal products, and is also obtained from the sun! Light skinned people need 15-20 minutes of sunshine on their face, hands, and arms, 2 to 3 times a week.

Vitamin B-12 is produced only by bacteria living in animals and the soil. You should eat plenty of lean meat and veggies to make sure you get enough.

Oils used in baking, in dressing, for sauteing and frying, their quality and nutritional value is an important but easily overlooked when considering a healthy diet. Many people are worried that oils will hurt them when it comes to controlling their weight. Do not think this way! Your body needs oil!

The Function of Oils

Fats are required in the diet as they provide the structural components of the cell walls of all tissues. They also act as carriers for the soluble vitamins A, D, E and K.

While an excess of saturated fat in the diet can lead to raised cholesterol levels and heart-related diseases, poly unsaturated fats can actually lower cholesterol levels. Some oils contain essential fatty acids, a deficiency of which can lead to heart disease, acne and eczema. Mono unsaturates have actually been found to reduce cholesterol levels.

How Do We Get our Oils?

Oil is extracted from the raw material by mechanical pressure (or in the case of refined oils, chemical solvents).

Where a product is soft, it is cold pressed, keeping vitamin destruction to a minimum.

Harder products such as safflower are expeller processed. Extraction rates from pressings are low and the oil has a higher nutritional value. It also retains its characteristic smell and taste.

Different Types of Oil to Use When Cooking

Olive Oil- the strength of its flavor lends itself to use as a salad dressing (add a little lemon juice or vinegar for extra "tang") or as a condiment with jacket potatoes, pizzas and hot vegetables. It can also be used in casseroles and in sauces.

Corn Oil- Use in baking or in salads.

Sesame oil- A favorite in Oriental cookery. It is usually fairly pungent in flavor, so is best used in small quantities. A favorite oil for stir-fries and marinades.

Nut oils are particularly good in salad dressing and vegetable dishes. Almond oil is ideal for use in cakes and pastries.

Choosing the Oil Best for You...

Commercial oils are highly processed, which means that much of the nutritional value is destroyed. Quality natural oils are only obtained by "cold pressing". This is a purely mechanical process, during which temperatures are maintained at a low level. There is no chemical or heat treatment.

Mechanical Pressing- Has an acidity of less than 1%. Likely to be the product of just one country or region. Flavor will be strong.

Extra Virgin First Pressed- This is the purest and finest oil and is extracted from the first pressing.

Extra Virgin Cold Pressed- Low pressure pressing. High quality.

Pure- Oil extracted from the third or fourth pressing and refined. The refining process includes washing with caustic soda, bleaching, fine filtering and deodorizing at high temperatures. These processes can remove minerals and vitamin E which is a natural antioxidant and prevents rancidification.

Light Last pressing. The mildest flavor.

VITAMIN DEFICIENCIES AND SIGNS OF EXCESS

You may be tempted to just eat terribly and try to fix it by giving yourself or your children a vitamin. While some vitamins are great, you need to know what you are doing, for excess vitamins can kill you!

This table lists the signs of vitamin under-and oversupply.

VITAMIN	Deficiency signs	Excess signs
Vitamin A	Night blindness, dry, rough skin, eye cornea thickening.	Yellowing of skin and eye whites; painful joint swellings; nausea; dry skin; elevated spinal fluid pressure.
Vitamin B1 (thiamine)	Fatigue, insomnia, irritability, loss of tenderness, lassitude, beriberi.	No side effects known from oral usage.
Vitamin B2 (riboflavin)	Mouth irritation, corner of mouth and lip cracking, magenta-colored tongue, dermatitis, eye redness, exaggerated sensitivity to light.	None known.
Vitamin B3 (niacin or niacinamide)	Loss of appetite, nervousness, mental depression, soreness and redness of the tongue, skin pigmentation,	Niacin excess can cause a temporary flushing of the skin, which is not known to be harmful thought to be beneficial.

	ulceration of the gums, diarrhea, pellagra.	
Vitamin B5 (pantothenic acid)	Headache, fatigue, muscle cramps, lack of coordination.	None known.
Vitamin B6 (pyridoxine)	Loss of appetite, diarrhea, skin and mouth disorders.	None known.
Vitamin B12 (cyanoco-balamin)	Anemia, degeneration of the nervous system.	None known.
Folic acid	Anemia, intestinal problems.	None known.
Biotin	Anemia, muscular pain, skin disorder.	None known.
Choline	None known.	None known.

Inositol	None known.	None known.
Para-aminobenzoic acid (PABA)	None known.	None known.
Vitamin C (ascorbic acid)	Bleeding and receding gums, unexplained bruises, slow healing, scurvy.	Diarrhea.
Vitamin D	Loss of appetite, cramps, poor bone formation, rickets.	Unusual thirst.urinary urgency vomiting, diarrhea.
Vitamin E (tocopherol)	Pigmentation, anemia-no specific deficiency disease recognized.	None known.
Vitamin K	Diarrhea, tendency to bleed.	None known, but abnormal clotting time may result.

From that list you will see that your body needs food in order to function properly. And eating the same thing day after day would cause you to become deathly ill! This is why we need to eat the right combinations of God's provisions.

A good basic plan to follow when feeding yourself, your future husband, and eventually your children might be the following:

Breads and Cereals (6 or more servings)
1 slice of bread
½ bagel
½ English Muffin
1 cup dry cereal
½ cup cooked cereal
½ cup rice

Vegetables (4 or more)
½ cup cooked vegetables or juice
1 cup raw vegetables

Fruits (3 or more)
1 medium piece
½ cup canned fruit or fruit juice
2 Tablespoons raisins

Legumes or Protein (2 to 3)
1 palm size patty of lean ground meat
2 slices of turkey breast
1/2 cup tuna fish
1- 3 oz. piece of beef
1 egg
1 - 3 oz. piece of chicken
Other 3 oz. meat items
1 cup of milk (preferably low-fat)
1 - 2 oz. slice of cheese

1/2 cup of cottage cheese
1 cup of lowfat yogurt
1 cup soy milk
½ cup cooked dry beans or peas
4 ounces tofu or tempeh
1 vegan burger patty

The Bible tells us that we are not to eat for just pleasure but for health's sake. But you should try with all your heart to please your family's taste buds. The reason being, in all honesty, if it doesn't taste good they won't eat it.

I'm sure that you have had food put before you that didn't appeal to your liking. Did you enjoy that meal? Probably not. Probably you just smeared it around your plate, making it look as if you had eaten a bit of it. You might have left the table preferably being hungry rather than shoveling even one bite into your mouth!

Well, if you are the cook, you should try your best to not have your children feel that way about your cooking.

You can make delicious, healthy meals, and now is the time to start learning how!

The following portion of this chapter we are going to learn how to cook your favorite fast food at home. Fast food, such as McDonald's, Burger King, Kentucky Fried Chicken, Taco Bell, and others may taste good, but it is awfully expensive and may not be that good for you. You can cook your favorite food at home for only a portion of the money you would spend eating out. In fact, you could cook those items for four days, for the price of eating out once!

Collecting Your Recipe Notebook

One of our daughter's favorite items to chose was her own Recipe Notebook. You can easily find a small, three-ring notebook at any Dollar Store for under $2. We did, however, expend $9 of her babysitting money to purchase a lovely Recipe Notebook from

Hallmark.

After purchasing your own three ring 6" x 6", or 5" x 6" notebook (the sizes will vary by an inch or so for the cover), you can use the following patterns for copying, and rather than spending a small fortune on refill pages, make your own recipe pages.

Important Note When Copying Patterns:

☞   For the recipe cards, use a light cover stock (ask them to help you at Office Depot or Office Max) for copying; not too heavy or it will jam the copying machine.

☞   For the refill pages for your notebook, use regular paper, but it's fun to use a variety of color for the different sections of your notebook. This makes it easy to find the recipe you are looking for.

☞   Make sure that you do it yourself at a local copy center, for if they do it, it is twice as much. As a future mother and homemaker, you will find that you will be at the copy center a lot! Learn now how to use the machines!

After copying this page, take it to Kinkos and for very small fee they will cut it in two and trim all the edges. You can also give these for gifts! (Fold in half and stick it in a recipe card holder)

Serves _____

Recipe Title: _____

Recipe From: _____

Ingredients: _____

Serves _____

Recipe Title: _____

Recipe From: _____

Ingredients: _____

Carefully cut each of these out and put them in your 3 - ring notebook under the correct section of food.

Serves: 4 (You can double or triple recipe as your family grows)

Recipe Title: Mock Big Mac

Ingredients:

2 cups shredded lettuce (only use romaine or other dark green type of lettuce, never iceberg. It has no nutritional value.)

1 lb. ground beef or ground turkey (buy the lowest in fat content)

1 sliced onion

1 sliced tomato

Thousand Island dressing (you can make this yourself by mixing 1/2 catsup to 1/2 mayo and a teaspoon and pickle relish)

1 package of hamburger buns - whole wheat are better for you - (you can freeze the left overs)

Make hamburger patties and cook them thoroughly. Place on hamburger bun and add the yummies. Homemade Big Macs are lower in fat and actually healthy for you!

Serves: 4 (You can double or triple recipe as your family grows)

Recipe Title: Mock Shaker Salads

Ingredients:

1 large bunch of butter or romaine lettuce, shredded

1 chopped tomato

Shredded parmesan or cheddar cheese

2 slices of turkey luncheon meat, sliced in strips

4 chopped green onions

Homemade Delicious Salad Dressing: (Thanks to Mary Greider!)

1 cup of Mayo

2 tablespoons of Rice Vinegar

Mix well. Add more vinegar to your personal taste.

In large Tupperware bowl with lid, shake all the salad ingredients together, then drizzle with dressing.

Serves: 4 (You can double or triple recipe as your family grows)

Recipe Title: Mock Taco Bell Tacos

Ingredients:

2 cups lettuce (only use romaine or other dark green type of lettuce, never iceburg. It has no nutritional value.)

1 lb. ground beef

1 chopped tomato

1 package taco seasoning (buy this in bulk from Costo or Sams)

1 cup shredded cheddar cheese

1 - 12 package of hard taco shells

Cook the ground beef and add your taco seasoning according to the directions. Layer it like Taco Bell does, meat mixture on the bottom, cheese, lettuce and tomato. If you want to make it a deluxe, add sour cream, and more tomatoes.

Serves: 4 (You can double or triple recipe as your family grows)

Recipe Title: Mock Taco Bell Burritos

Ingredients:

12 small wheat tortillas (we prefer the 96% fat free, whole wheat)

1 small jar of tomato salsa

1/4 cup of chopped onions

1 cup shredded cheddar cheese

1 can refried, fat free beans

Heat tortillas in the over wrapped in foil until they are warm. Heat the refried beans in a saucepan and add 3/4 cup of salsa. After it is warm, stir in chopped onions. Place bean mixture inside the tortillas and then top with cheese. Wrap!

Hint: Make sure that you do not purchase refried beans which contain lard. This will hurt your body.

Serves: 4 (You can double or triple recipe as your family grows)

Recipe Title: Homemade Yogurt Parfait

Ingredients:

1 large carton of fat free/lowfat vanilla yogurt
1 small package of frozen mixed berry fruit
1 small box of granola cereal

Take a large parfait cup (if you don't have one, simply use a large drinking glass), and layer it with yogurt, fruit, yogurt, fruit, yogurt, ending with granola on top. Leave out for one hour in order for berries to defrost.

A great breakfast treat that is very healthy for you!

Serves: 4 (You can double or triple recipe as your family grows)

Recipe Title: The Best Milk Shakes in the World!

Ingredients:

1 frozen carton of fat free/lowfat ice-cream or frozen yogurt
Skim or lowfat milk
Flavoring: Either frozen berries of some sort; bananas; chocolate syrup and a tablespoon of peanut butter; or all of the above!

In blender, scoop desired amount of ice cream, about four scoops (one scoop per person), pour 4 cups of milk, and then add your flavoring. If it doesn't blend well, you haven't poured enough milk, so add a little more to get it really blending well. Mmmmm! Another great breakfast, all in a glass!

Serves: 4 (You can double or triple recipe as your family grows)

Recipe Title: Move over Olive Garden! Mama Mia's Favorite Spaghetti Sauce

Ingredients:

1 large institutional can of tomato sauce
1 large institutional can of crushed tomatoes
2 teaspoons of crushed garlic
2 teaspoons of sugar
2 chopped onions
2 chopped green peppers
1/4 cup Italian seasoning (you can buy this is bulk from Sams or Costco) Our family prefers the spicy kind.
2 large cans of sliced mushrooms, drained

In 2 tablespoons of olive oil, simmer garlic, onions and green peppers. When tender add the rest of ingredients and simmer on low for 8 hours, stirring every half hour. Best served over spaghetti noodles with Romano cheese sprinkled over the top.

Serves: 4 (You can double or triple recipe as your family grows)

Recipe Title: Healthy Vegetable Lasagna

Ingredients:

Whole Wheat Lasagna noodles
Use the left over sauce for spaghetti from the previous page
8 cups of steamed Normandy Mix (from Sams - has frozen broccoli, squash, carrots and cauliflower in one large bag)
4 cups of lowfat cottage cheese & lowfat mozzarella cheese

Cook lasagna noodles in boiling water until tender (do not overcook or they get mushy). In a large lasagna pan, layer first with sauce, next a layer of noodles; then, all cottage cheese; vegetables; sauce; noodles; 2 c. mozzarella; vegetables; sauce; noodles; then remaining mozzarella cheese. Bake in a 350 degree oven for 35 minutes. You can freeze the leftovers in freezer baggies.

Carefully cut each of these out and put them in your 3 - ring notebook under the correct section of food.

Recipe Title: Real Kentucky Fried Chicken

Serves: 4 *(You can double or triple recipe as your family grows)*

Ingredients:

4 large, skinless chicken breasts
1/2 cup olive oil
1 cup flour seasoned with lots of salt and pepper
3 beaten eggs

Take the chicken breasts and dip them in the eggs. Next, roll them in the seasoned flour. In large skillet, heat oil on medium high and then place the breasts in the oil to cook. Cover for five minutes at this heat and then turn breasts over. Cook for another five minutes on medium high and then turn to simmer. Simmer each side for 20 minutes. Finger lickin' good!!!! Serve with the mashed potatoes and gravy on next page.

Recipe Title: The Best Mashed Potatoes & Gravy

Serves: 8 *(You can double or triple recipe as your family grows)*

Ingredients:

POTATOES

8 peeled potatoes
1 peeled rutabaga
1/4 cup butter
1 cup milk
Salt & Pepper

GRAVY

4 chicken bouillon cubes
4 cups water
1/8 cup corn starch

Cook potatoes & rutabaga in water until tender. Mash and then slowly add the rest of the ingredients. Beat with a beater until fluffy. For gravy, bring water & bouillon cubes to boil. Mix corn starch with a little cold water & pour into boiling mix. Stir until thick.

Serves: 16 (Freeze leftovers in freezer baggies for lunches)

Recipe Title: The Original Chicken Noodle Soup

Ingredients:

4 lg., skinless, boneless chicken breasts, cooked & chopped

1/4 cup olive oil

8 carrots, peeled & chopped

8 stalks of celery, chopped

2 chopped onions

12 bouillon cubes

12 cups of water

1 package of spaghetti noodles, broken in small pieces

In very large pot, cook onions, carrots & celery in olive oil until almost tender. Add water & bouillon cubes, chicken & bring to a boil. Add noodles & cook for another 10 minutes. Bring to a simmer for 20 minutes until noodles are tender.

Serves: 16 (Freeze remaining servings in freezer bags)

Recipe Title: Beef Stew With Vegetables

Ingredients:

1 pound of stew meat, cut small

2 chopped onions

8 chopped & peeled carrots

8 chopped celery stalks

1 small package frozen green beans

4 potatoes, peeled and chopped

12 beef bouillon cubes

12 cups water

1/2 cup corn starch

Cook meat until tender. Add vegetables & sauté 10 minutes. Add water and bouillon cubes. Bring to boil for 10 minutes and then simmer for about 4 hours. When meat & veggies are all very tender, bring to boil & add corn starch liquefied with a little cold water.

Stir until thick.

Serve with fresh bread.

Serves: 6

Recipe Title: Sukiyaki

Ingredients:

Oil for frying

1 tsp. sesame oil

1/2 lb. beef, cut
in small pieces

1 small sweet potato,
peeled & sliced thin

1 white turnip, peeled
& sliced thin

1 lb. sliced mushrooms

1/4 cup chicken broth

1/2 lb. Chinese cabbage, shred-
ed

3 tablespoons soy sauce

3 cups hot cooked rice

1/2 lb. tofu cut in small pieces

Sauce to Dip: 1/2 cup each of soy sauce, lime juice &
semisweet cooking sherry. Mix well.

In large fry pan, cook meat in oil until cooked. Add all
veggies & broth except cabbage. Cover & steam until
tender. Add soy sauce, cabbage, & tofu. Stir fry until
tender. Serve with rice & sauce. Very, very good & 1/8
the cost of restaurant Sukiyaki.

Serves: 4

Recipe Title: Chinese Curried Chicken With
Noodles

Ingredients:

1 8 oz. package rice noodles

1/2 tsp. salt

Olive & Sesame Oil

1 small purple onion, chopped

2 cups water

1/2 cup catsup

1 tsp. Worcester Sauce

1/2 tsp. salt

1/2 tsp. sugar

1 tablespoon curry powder

1/2 cup chicken broth

2 cups chopped, cooked
chicken

1 tomato, cut in wedges

Drop noodles into boiling salted water. Add a few drops
sesame oil & cook till tender. Drain, place on platter after
tossing with a little more oil. Mix together catsup, Worc.
sauce, 1/2 tsp. salt & sugar. In hot skillet or wok, add
curry powder & then broth. Turn to high. Add onion &
chicken. Bring to a boil. Stir in the catsup mix. Add tomato
wedges. Stir until heated.
Serve over noodles.

Serves: 6

Recipe Title: Fruit Salad Dessert

Ingredients:

1 cup sour cream (you can substitute lowfat or fat free)
1 cup pineapple chunks, drained
1 cup miniature marshmallows
1 cup shredded coconut
1 cup mandarin orange slices (drained)

Mix together all the ingredients and allow to marinate together overnight in the refrigerator. It will be a family favorite. Your husband and children will eat it and want more!

Serves: 8

Recipe Title: Cole Slaw ¿ Sweet ¿ Sour
Salad Dressing

Ingredients:

1/2 head of chopped cabbage
1 tomato chopped finely
1/2 green pepper, chopped very finely
1/4 cup of red onion, chopped finely

Dressing:

1/4 cup vinegar
1 teaspoon of garlic salt
1/8 cup of sugar
Shake together in claret

Add:

1/8 cup of olive oil

Mix ¿ pour over cole slaw.

Serves: 6

Recipe Title: Homemade Honey Wheat Bread

Ingredients:

1 1/8 cup lukewarm water

2 1/2 cups unbleached flour

1/2 cups whole wheat bread flour

1 1/2 tablespoon of dry milk (powdered milk)

1 1/2 tablespoon of honey

2 tablespoons of butter

2 teaspoons fast rising yeast (or 3 teaspoons active dry)

Let yeast dissolve in lukewarm water. Add the rest of the ingredients and knead until very elastic. Cover & allow to rise for one hour. Punch & knead again. Place in two bread tins and let rise. Bake at 350 degrees for 20-30 minutes until brown and fragrant odor is all through your house.

Serves: 8

Recipe Title: Healthy-Nut Bread

Ingredients:

1/1/3 cups lukewarm water

3 cups whole wheat flour

1 1/2 teaspoons of Salt

2 tablespoons of Honey

2 tablespoons of Molasses

1 Tablespoon of Gluten

2 Tablespoons of Olive Oil

2/3 cups Seeds (Sunflower, Flax, or pumpkin does fine)

3 teaspoons of active dry Yeast

Dissolve yeast in lukewarm water. Add the remaining ingredients except the seeds. Knead well and then add the seeds. Cover and let rise for one hour. Punch down. Knead again for a few minutes, separate and place in two greased bread pans. Cover, allow to rise, and then bake in 350 degree oven. Bake for 20-30 minutes.

Serves: 6

Recipe Title: Broccoli Corn Bread

Thank you, Mary Greider!

Ingredients:

1 package of Jiffy corn bread mix
3 eggs
1/4 cup oil
1 cup cottage cheese
1 cup frozen chopped broccoli

Mix all ingredients together and place in a greese square pan. Bake at 350 degrees for 20-25 minutes until thoroughly cooked. This is a melt in your mouth recipe and you can double it and serve it for lunch the next day! Great way to get the little ones to eat their broccoli!

Serves: 8

Recipe Title: Gingerbread Mix (keeps 6 months) Gingerbread Recipe following

Ingredients:

2 cups sugar
8 cups unbleached flour
1/4 cup baking powder
2 1/2 tsp. salt
1 tsp. baking soda
1 tsp. cloves

3 tblsp. ground ginger
3 tblsp. cinnamon
2 1/4 cups vegetable shortening

Mix all the dry ingredients together. Cut in the shortening with a pastry cutter until it is crumbly. Store it in ziplock baggies with no air inside. Keep it in your cellar where it is cool and dry.

Gingerbread: Mix 1 egg, 1/2 cup boiling water, 1/2 cup molasses ; then add 2 1/2 cups of mix. Pour inter a greased and floured square pan and bake at 350 degrees for 20 minutes.

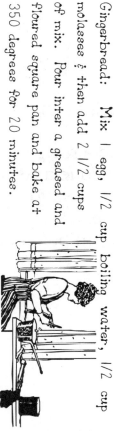

Categorizing Your Recipe Notebook

There are different categories for listing your recipes:

☞ Vegetables

☞ Appetizers

☞ Beverages

☞ Breads

☞ Casseroles/Main Dishes

☞ Desserts

☞ Meat/Poultry/Fish

☞ Soups/Salads

☞ Miscellaneous

Under each different topic, place your favorite recipes that you find.

When you are eating at friend's homes and you find a recipe that you love, a hostess is always truly honored when someone asks for a recipe that she has made. Don't be embarrassed to ask for it!

Place your recipe notebook in an easy to locate place in your hope chest. You will be using it again and again, as you pull it out to enter recipes that you will find.

CHAPTER TEN

ꕥ *House Cleaning* ꕥ

"Cleanliness is next to Godliness..."

You will find that one of the most important things to learn when you are young is that of efficiently cleaning a home. We have already talked about how if a home is not kept clean, illnesses and germs will spread!

The following items should be placed in your hope chest and taken out to be studied and memorized:

~ A cleaning check list which you can copy and edit during your cleaning lifetime.

~ A list of cleansing solutions which will help in keeping your household items looking brand new!

~ A list of necessary cleaning items which you will need to have in your home to help keep the household clean.

It isn't difficult to clean a home. The first thing to remember is what hundreds of helpful cleaning books will tell you...

DO NOT CLUTTER YOUR HOME!

Keep your home free of excess items and debris. We have already discussed the issue of how we should have a place for everything and everything in its place. When you go to clean your room or your home, it is very necessary to have everything picked up and organized. How difficult would it be to vacuum your room if all your belongings were scattered all over it? It would be very hard! This same principle goes towards a home which has too many things with no real place where those things belong. It makes it almost impossible to get really clean.

One thing to think about as you start your cleaning chores is to remember how easy we have it in the 2000's. Unlike our ancestors who had to use lots and lots of elbow grease to wash clothes with a wash board, we have a washing machine and dryer! We also have modern conveniences such as dishwashers, ovens, microwaves, running water and more! Think of how much time these wonderful inventions have saved the common housewife.

Did you know that because most of our woodwork is painted glossy, that this has even cut down the modern housekeeper's work? In the past, when unfinished wood was used in homes, it was almost impossible to dust it clean as we can today.

Cleaning Chart

The chart on the following page is a simple list that you may wish to photocopy and place in a folder and title it "house cleaning". You can use this and continue to place useful information inside. Place it in your hope chest to use when you have your own home.

You don't have to do every chore on the list weekly.

Some cleaning only has to be done monthly or even every other month, such as washing and ironing the curtains. Also note that some curtains can only be dry cleaned. Be very careful when washing your curtains as some may shrink if you try to do it in your wash machine.

This list has been invaluable to many women as sometimes it is easy to forget to do something and then they wonder why every one in the home is sneezing, and they don't have colds...

Make one or more copies (depending on who else is helping) and check what you want done.

Happy cleaning!...

CLEANING LIST

Kitchen:

___ Clean outside of cupboards
___ Oven
   ___ inside ___ outside
___ Refridgerator
   ___ inside ___ outside
___ Sinks, scoured
___ Floors
   ___ swept ___ mopped ___ waxed
___ Windows washed
___ Freezer, defrosted & cleaned
___ Hallways
   ___ swept ___ mopped ___ waxed
___ Clean windowsills

Dining Area:

___ Dining table scrubbed & disinfected
___ Chairs scrubbed & disinfected
___ Chair covers washed, dried & ironed
___ Rugs washed & air dried
___ Carpet vacuumed
___ Carpet spot cleaned
___ Dusted
___ Dust baseboards
___ Vacuum curtains
___ Wash & iron curtains
___ Clean windowsills

Family Room:

___ Dust all metal & glass furniture & objects

Bathroom:

___ Oil dust all wood furniture
___ Wash windows
___ Move furniture & vacuum
___ Vacuum floor
___ Vacuum couch & other cloth furniture
___ Dust baseboards
___ Wash any blankets or afghans
___ Feather dust lampshades
___ Vacuum curtains
___ Wash & iron curtains
___ Clean windowsills
___ Scour sink
___ Scrub & scour toilet
___ Scrub tub
___ Clean & buff sink area & faucets
___ Clean & polish mirrors
___ Sweep floors
___ Mop floors
___ Wax floors
___ Wash fixtures
___ Dust bathroom decor
___ Dust baseboards
___ Vacuum floor
___ Clean windowsills

Bedrooms:

___ Change bed linens
___ Vacuum floors
___ Move furniture & vacuum under
___ Dust glass & metal furniture

Other:

___ Dust & water plants

Living Room:

___ Oil dust wood furniture
___ Dust & clean windowsill
___ Polish mirrors
___ Feather dust lampshades
___ Vacuum curtains
___ Wash & iron curtains
___ Clean baseboards
___ Dust glass & metal furniture
___ Oil dust wood furniture
___ Vacuum cloth furniture
___ Move furniture & vacuum under
___ Vacuum curtains
___ Wash & iron curtains
___ Feather dust knick-knacks
___ Feather dust lamp shades

_____
_____
_____
_____
_____
_____
_____
_____

CLEANSERS:

AMMONIA: Most of the cleansers on the store shelves are nothing but ammonia. Purchase a large bottle for under $2 and simply use it diluted with water. For a strong cleanser use one cup per gallon of water. For a great mild cleanser use 1/2 cup per gallon. We use this solution for our dirty kitchen and bathroom floors, or any other area with linoleum. We also use it on kitchen counters which have some stubborn stains.

BLEACH: Bleach is a great cleaner for the tub with tiles that are accumulating mildew. Get a spray bottle and carefully label it BLEACH. Spray the straight bleach on the tiled area and scrub. Rinse thoroughly. Store away from children. You can also use bleach, VERY CAREFULLY, on a very stubborn stain in clothing. Take a tiny drop and place it on the stain. Watch until it is gone and then rinse ALL the bleach from the fabric. Leaving any in at all on the fabric will cause it to simply melt away leaving a large hole.

APPLE CIDER VINEGAR: Believe it or not, apple cider vinegar is one of the best cleaners you can have in a household. Use it to clean your refrigerator, your coffee maker and those stubborn pans. Fill your coffee maker with 1/3 cup of vinegar and 1 pot of water. Run through. If that doesn't get the stains soak the pieces in pure vinegar until they are gone. It is mild yet powerful cleanser. Vinegar also cleans copper. Just for fun, try soaking your pans with a copper bottom and see what happens. Voila! A shine like you've never seen before!

THE ULTIMATE HOMEMADE CLEANSER FOR EVERYTHING

Cally Thompson has used this for years and has given us permission to give this cleanser recipe for you to use.

1/3 cup ammonia
1/2 cup vinegar
1 1/2 Tbsp baking soda
1 gallon water

This cleanser is great for all cleaning jobs in the home. If you want it stronger, simply double the recipe. Avoid the fumes.

DRAIN CLEANER

My grandmother gave me this recipe for unclogging drains. Long before Drano or any other de-clogger, women used this simple solution with normal household products.

All you do is pour 1 cup of baking soda into the clogged drain. Next pour 1 cup of apple cider vinegar down the drain. Let it fizzle for a while and then turn the hot water faucet on and let run for a while. This is much safer for the family with little children than those that contain dangerous and harmful chemicals.

All of these cleansers are inexpensive and easy to use. Try them on your bathroom and objects now, and take joy in keeping clean!

OLD ENGLISH FURNITURE OIL: There are different types of this wonderful product, a light lemon colored oil for polishing, and a dark oil for fixing scratches. Purchase the buffing oil and follow the directions on the bottle. Wood needs to be taken care of in order for it to last a long time. When moving from a dry climate to a wet one, your wood will blister and swell or dry up and crack depending on which way you move. In order to protect your wood furniture from the environment, you must preserve it with this product.

MURPHY'S OIL SOAP: This product is a must for all kitchens with wood cupboards. Follow the directions on the back of the bottle and use it to clean your cupboards. It isn't harsh and will protect the wood. Follow up after it is clean and dry with the Old English Oil. This will make your cupboards shine and also will help them to last a lifetime or longer!

WINDEX IS SIMPLY AMMONIA: We already touched on the issue of ammonia and how to use it. Windex is simply touched up ammonia. Spray your ammonia solution on your windows and use old newspapers which are dry to clean and buff them until they shine. Many a bird has had a climatic ending with women who use this technique! (They fly right into it because they can't see the window it is so clean.)

AJAX CLEANSER WITH BLEACH: Every household isn't complete until they have Ajax Cleanser in their home. Use this product on tubs, toilets, kitchen sinks and where other nasty stains accumulate. Sprinkle, let it sit. Scrub and rinse. Looks like brand new!

CLEANING SUPPLIES:

~ Cloth baby diapers (for dusting, etc.)
~ Newspaper (for cleaning & buffing glass and chrome)
~ Old towel rags (for cleaning)
~ Mop
~ Broom & Dust pan
~ Vacuum and attachments for thorough cleaning
~ Pails for water & cleaning solutions
~ Feather duster
~ Scratcher sponge (scratcher on one side, sponge on reverse)

VACUUM

One of the most important investments in your home will be your vacuum. The one most people have been happiest with in their homes, and which has been voted the most effective, is the ORECK brand vacuum cleaner.

An Oreck will cost approximately $200, but it is well worth the price you pay and will help keep down your medical expenses if you have allergies. Merry Maids and other cleaning companies use Oreck vacuum cleaners because they have the most power and yet are the lightest and place the least amount of stress on the homemaker's back.

There are many other vacuums available at Kmart and other variety stores, but after hearing many personal testimonies of how much better the Oreck's vacuums have cleaned carpets, we would suggest that you start saving your money now to have one for your own home. It is worth it.

One small tip... When cleaning your house always remember to vacuum first and then dust. The reason being that you spread dust when vacuuming. If you dust first, you have to do it immediately after vacuuming because some dust always escapes from the exhaust fan in the motor.

Stain Removal Tips:

BLOOD: When you find blood on a fabric, immediately run it under cold water, and soap it. Rinse all the soap out. Then soak the stain in a solution of 2 tablespoons of ammonia to 1 gallon of cool water. If a stain still remains, you may want to try straight bleach, but be very careful. If it is left too long it will eat your fabric right away.

ANTIPERSPIRANT: We would urge all ladies to use only deodorant crystals from your local health food store which do not contain aluminum. You have read previously the danger of aluminum in the previous chapters. The deodorant crystals do not stain your clothing either. If you use the other and it stains your clothing rub liquid laundry detergent into the stain and wash out. Rinse.

BUTTER: Dropped some butter onto your new dress at the dining table? Purchase a dry-cleaning solvent at your local grocery store and wash with warm water. Rinse.

COFFEE or TEA: Immediately after a spill soak the fabric in cool water and then scrub the area after placing liquid detergent immediately on your stain. Rinse. If it is a stubborn stain use a watered down bleach solution, *carefully*.

INK: When a toddler starts to create on clothing it may seem that it is there to stay. You can get rid of ink stains by sponging it out with rubbing alcohol. If it is a type of permanent ink marker, use an ammonia solution such as what you will use with blood. When you launder, make sure that you pour 1 cup of bleach into the wash water (as long as it is not a colored load!).

GUM: Have you ever had the misfortune to sit on gum? How do you get it out of your skirt? Take an ice cube and harden the gum. Next, scrape off as much as you can with a dinner knife. To get rid of the rest of the gum, soak it in a dry-cleaning solvent and then scrape the remaining off.

CHOCOLATE: This may seem like an impossible stain, but use the ammonia solution which you use with blood. If a bit of a stain remains, apply dry-cleaning solvent and rinse out. Then wash with 1 cup of bleach in your machine wash water.

GREASE: You can get out oil stains by using a dry-cleaning solvent. Then after it is rinsed, use a pre-wash stain remover and wash in your machine in hot water.

PERSPIRATION: Yellow under the arm pits? Pour a bit of liquid detergent into the stain and then let it sit over night. Wash as you would normally do. If there is discoloration of your fabric, hold the stain over the top of an ammonia bottle. You can also dab on white vinegar. If an alarming odor is still coming out of the material, soak it for 3 hours in a quart of water with 1/4 cup of salt.

URINE: Boys will be boys, and little guys never smell too sweet in the morning. To get rid of a urine stain in the rinse cycle use an ammonia solution which is 2 tablespoons of ammonia per cup of water. (Do not EVER use ammonia on wool items.)

GRASS: This stain is an every day occurrence with little boys in spring and summer. Use a liquid enzyme detergent, pouring it directly on the stain. Wash as usual with a color safe bleach product.

This list will help you throughout your lifetime. Don't throw away clothing that you think is ruined because of a stubborn stain. A little elbow grease and the right stain solution will help you to preserve the clothing that you have and keep them bright and new looking!

Preparing For House Work

Right now is the time to start learning how to become very capable house keepers. There is nothing more satisfying than cleaning up a home, and then sitting and relaxing, looking at the fruit of your hands.

There are scriptures regarding laziness which you probably have already read. You might like to memorize the following:

"I went by the field of the slothful (lazy), and by the vineyard of the man void of understanding; and, lo, it was all grown over with thorns, and nettles had covered the face thereof, and the stone wall thereof was broken down. Then I saw and considered it well. I looked upon it and received instruction. Yet a little sleep, a little slumber, a little folding of the hands to sleep. So shall thy poverty come as one that travelleth; and thy want as an armed man." Proverbs 24:30-34

"By much slothfulness (laziness) the building decayeth; and through idleness of the hands the house droppeth through." Ecclesiastics 10:18

I'm sure that there are times when none of us want to do something. Maybe the task looks overwhelming, or we are too tired to even start. But remember that we are to do all things as unto the Lord. Even our house cleaning!

Start now making a notebook with all the cleaning information you will need when you are married. Take notes on your stain removal solutions and on what works and what doesn't. If you find a wonderful cleaning item that you like, write it down. This is for your future as a wife and mother. Your husband and children will thank you! Then you will also have a tool (your notebook) to help your own daughters when they grow up.

Keep this information in your hope chest and constantly work on perfecting your skills.

CHAPTER ELEVEN

∽ *Frugality* ∽

"She considers a field and buyeth it; with the fruit of her hands she planteth a vineyard."
Proverbs 31: 16

Frugality sounds like a big word. It means that a person is "frugal", which is another way of saying that you are able to make a penny go a long way.

Studying frugality is one of the most important lessons in the area of homemaking. If you are obedient to God's Word, and choose to follow the satifying and wonderful path of being a "keeper at home" as the Scriptures tell us to be, then learning as much as you can about being frugal is a must.

When you get married, chances are that your new husband will make an average and modest income in the beginning. It will be your duty to take the household money that he will provide for you and make sure that you are able to obtain all the items that you need for your homemaking.

You do not want to be one of these women who do not know how to budget! They are given a certain amount of money from their husbands to purchase food and household needs and yet they spend it on a new dress for themselves and then whine to the husband that he hasn't given her enough money and so the family eats bean soup over and over again that paycheck period.

You want to be a woman that is very capable of finding the best cost for the items that you need. You must be able to determine a need from a want. You also need to be able to say "no", both to yourself and to your future children over unnecessary spending.

This is frugality!

You Do Not Make More Money Working!

It is important that we touch on a subject that you will be faced with all your life...

You will see throughout your lifetime as a mother and keeper of your home that the majority of women who are of the world, go out and provide for their families in the work force.

Do not be deceived into thinking that this is normal or even that a woman providing for her family actually make more money!

In actuality, women who go to work spend all the money they make and are not ahead monetarily over those mothers who stay home and do not work professionally.

Consider the following information....

Here is the truth of the matter:

Per Month Cost	Staying At Home	Working
Baby-sitting:	$0	$460
($115 per week per child)		
Work Clothing:	$0	$150
Fast Food:	$0	$40

(The average working family eats out at least twice a week, PLUS their regular grocery bill.)

Doctor Bills:	$0	$50

(It has been proven that those parents who have their children in day care spend more money on health care because of the easy transmission of flu and other germs in that environment. Also a mother at home is able to cook nutritious food as a working mother is not.)

Automobile:	$0	$150

(It is necessary to purchase another reliable car so that mother can drive to work.)

Gas:	$20	$120

(Based on a med. car)

Total expenditures:		$970

So, you are paying $970 a month (this is if you only have ONE young child) in order to go to work!

How much better to just stay at home and raise the wonderful children that God will give you? Save money, stay healthier and happier by doing things God's way rather than the world's!

Being a Mother to Your Children at Home

There are many young ladies who were trained in some profession, that choose to give up their career and take up the much more satifying occupation of mother! Many women who were nurses, doctors, lawyers, teachers, etc., quit those occupations because they realized it was simply a dead end job compared to rewarding job motherhood.

When you are submitted to the Lord and His Word, then you will want to do things as God says to do.

Today women are having children but allowing other people to raise them for them. This should not be! Being a mother is about nurturing your children, no matter what their age! Staying home is about being there for your children, at all hours of the day and night, when *they need you*.

Staying home with your children means doing your best as you rely on the Lord every day, to raise them into happy, healthy, responsible children and not giving that job over to someone else.

When you allow someone who is "paid" to take care of your children, they are only doing it for the money, not for the love of your children. The only person who can take care of your children properly is you!

It will be a lot of work. It will take time, patience and a lot of dying to self. But the Scriptures tell us that "women will be saved through childbearing". In the Greek that word doesn't mean the simple act of having the children physically. It literally means the TRAINING of those children.

You need to know now that being a mother isn't just meeting the physical needs of your children. Being a mother means that you are there for all their emotional and spiritual needs also. Constantly training and guiding them in the ways of the Lord rather than the ways of the world.

Many people view success by measuring how many material belongings they have in this world. This is why they send their wives out to work and they also work; sending the children to others for their child training. They may have big houses, drive expensive cars and have fancy clothing and household items, but I can assure you that chances are they do not have what counts... a true relationship with their children!

Statistics show that working parents are only in their homes (not counting sleep) three hours a day per work week, and only five hours on the weekend. So much for having big expensive houses if you never can live in them. This is a scary statistic! If working parents are only home three hours a day per week, how much of that time is spent with their children? Again, statistics show that parents are neglecting their children. They RARELY spend any amount of time with their children beyond tending to their physical needs!

And sad to say, many married couples are living in huge houses that could house ten children, and yet they don't have any!

Staying at home to raise your children is well worth any sacrifice of material goods. Because you can't take those with you when you die, but you CAN take your children, as you will all meet in Heaven for those who love the Lord!

Start a Frugal Notebook

1. Get yourself another 3 ring notebook and stock it with paper and dividers with pockets. This will be where you place your coupons for each area.

2. Divide your notebook into the following areas:

~Kitchen	~Children	~Automobile
~Cleaners	~Toiletries	~Entertainment
~Household	~Automobile	~School

You may think of more as time goes on, and then simply add it to notebook, making its own section.

Use this notebook to gather coupons, to write down or photo-copy money saving ideas that you will find. Also use it for a valuable resource guide by writing down addresses and phone numbers for resources that are free. We will list at the end of this book invaluable web pages that offer ideas and more resources for you to read.

You will use this notebook and coupon divider idea throughout your whole lifetime and it should be placed in your hope chest where you can access it easily.

You may wish to photocopy the following ideas and place them in your notebook under the correct area.

Frugal Shopping Tips

~ Buy items when they are on sale. Purchase a case if you can afford it for that way, sometimes you can save 50% on items that you would usually buy anyway.

~ Always look at the "COST PER UNIT" label under the item on a shelf when you are deciding which item is the least expensive to buy.

~ NEVER, EVER shop when you are hungry. You will end up purchasing a lot more than you need.

~ Try to always use coupons and only shop at the stores which offer double coupons.

~ Make sure that you check the register and that you are charged correctly. It is estimated that the grocery stores make $1000's a year, not purposely of course, through errors on the part of the cashiers.

~ Avoid too much red meat. This costs way too much and it has been reported that too much red meat is not good for us. Everything in moderation. Eating red meat once or twice a week will also cut down on the food budget.

~ When you do buy red meat, such as ground beef, buy it in bulk from places such as Sams or Costco. You will save half the cost you would pay if you went to a regular grocery store. Divide into sections and place in freezer baggies and then freeze.

~ Try not to eat out more than twice a month, and then eat at very inexpensive places. You can purchase a healthy chicken salad at McDonald's for under $3.

~ When you do go out to a restaurant, only go for the lunch

menu as it is almost half the cost of the regular dinner. For example, going to the Olive Garden and ordering a pasta and sauce only costs $5.49 which includes the salad and bread sticks. Dinner for the same comes to $8.95.

~ Check out K-mart and other variety stores for their specials on food. (By the way, in our area Safeway owns K-mart.) You can find your snack items such as cereal and chips on sale for a dollar a bag or box!

~ When traveling with kids either on a long trip or even on a short trip to the local zoo, always take a small food cooler. There have been many families who have their food cart with which they travel everywhere. They load it up with crackers for the toddlers, water bottles or juice for the little ones, whole wheat pretzels and dried beef for the teenagers. When they become hungry, rather than pull into the local fast food restaurant, they simply head for the food cooler. This saves hundreds of dollars each year for large families.

~ Rather than purchasing quick mix meals at the store. Make your own. We will give you a list of homemade mixes to make at the end of this section.

~ Buy your fruits and vegetables from Sams or Costco-like stores. You will save money as they purchase them in bulk and then pass on the savings to you.

~ Plan a menu. Do not wait until 4:00 and then decide that you will make dinner. Start helping your mother right now with the menu planning and help her make up a weekly and then monthly menu. This is the beginning for really saving money. Then you always know what you need and what you must buy.

All of these ideas are just the beginning for you! As you talk with your mother and your dear sisters in Christ, you will be adding more and more to your notebook daily. You will find as you save money and discover more ways to save , that it brings a satisfaction to know that you received more for your money than if you weren't thoughtful regarding thrifty and frugal ideas.

Homemade Mixes

All of the following mixes are to be stored in an air tight container in a cool, dry place. One substitute you may use is by using the Butter flavored Crisco or other brand of shortening. It really helps in the cookie mixes. They keep up to six months.

Chocolate Chip Cookie Mix

18 cups of unbleached flour
3 tablespoons baking soda
1 1/2 tablespoons salt
6 cups brown sugar
6 cups white sugar
8 cups shortening
10 cups chocolate chips (you can purchase a large bag at your local Sams or Costco)

Place dry ingredients in bowl, add shortening and mix, don't be afraid to get your hands dirty! Add nuts and chocolate.

To make: 8 cups of Mix with 2 teaspoon vanilla with 2 eggs. Bake in 350 degree oven for 10-15 minutes for medium size cookies.

Brownie Mix

8 cups sugar
1 tablespoon salt

4 cups flour
2 1/2 cups shortening
3 cups unsweetened cocoa

This mix will make 3 oblong

pans of brownies for your family.

To make: Mix 4 eggs with 2 teaspoons vanilla. Beat in 5 cups of Brownie Mix. Add nuts as desired. Bake in a 350 degree oven for 35-40 minutes. Cool and cut.

Healthy Pancake Mix

4 cups whole wheat flour
4 cups white flour
1/4 cup baking powder
2 tablespoons baking soda
1/4 cup sugar
2 teaspoons salt

Mix all ingredients together. This mix keeps up to nine months!

To make: 2 cups Mix, 2 eggs separated (beat the egg whites till stiff), 2 cups buttermilk, 1/4 cup olive oil. Combine everything but egg whites. After blended, fold in beaten egg whites. Cook on hot griddle. Serve with syrup.

Cheese Mix for Mac & Cheese & Helpers

4 cups of unbleached flour
15 cups dried grated Parmesan cheese
16 cups powdered milk
1/4 cup salt
2 tablespoons paprika
4 cups butter, pebbled with pastry cutter

Mix everything but butter and then cut in the butter with your pastry cutter until it is coarse but fine. This must be stored in the refrigerator or freezer in baggies. Will keep for 7 months.

To make: With a whisk, blend 1 cup of the mix and 2 cups of milk in a saucepan until it comes to a boil. Reduce and simmer.

Macaroni & Cheese with Cheese Mix

4 cups elbow macaroni
2 cups Cheese Mix

Cook macaroni until tender in boiling water. In another saucepan, with a whisk, combine mix with 2 cups of water and 2 cups of milk. After thickens, pour into drained macaroni.

Mom's Helper for Hamburger with Cheese Mix

1 lb. of cooked hamburger
4 cups elbow macaroni
1/4 cup minced dried onion
1 small can of tomato paste
2 cups Cheese Mix
(plus 2 cups water and 2 cups milk)

After meat is brown and drained, add macaroni, onion, tomato paste and Cheese Mix to large skillet. Add 2 cups of water and 2 cups of milk. Bring to boil and immediately cover and then reduce heat to simmer. Let cook for 45 minutes until macaroni is tender.

Mom's Tuna Helper with Cheese Mix

4 cups of thin egg noodles
1/4 cup dried minced onions
1 cup diced celery
3 cans tuna
2 cups Cheese Mix
2 cups water
2 cups milk

Add all ingredients to large skillet, bring to boil, cover and then simmer until noodles are tender. Serve with salad or other vegetable.

Variety Cookie Mix

18 cups of unbleached flour
2 tablespoons baking soda
1 1/2 tablespoons salt
8 cups shortening
6 cups sugar
6 cups brown sugar

Mix all dry ingredients *thoroughly*. Cut in shortening until crumbly. Keeps 4 months.

Gingersnaps

4 cups Cookie Mix
1/2 cup molasses
2 teaspoons vanilla
2 beaten eggs
1 teaspoon of ginger
1 teaspoon cinnamon
1 teaspoon allspice
1/4 teaspoon cloves

To make: Mix all ingredients and place quarter size pieces of dough on the cookie sheet. Bake at 350 degrees for about 10 minutes. Approximately 24 cookies.

Sugar Cookies

6 cups Cookie Mix
3 teaspoons vanilla
2 eggs

Mix all ingredients with 1 tablespoon of milk. For a fun effect, take a bowl of sugar, after rolling your dough into a ball, roll it into the sugar. Take a fork and press down. Bake at 350 degrees for 10 minutes until lightly brown on edges.

Peanut Butter Cookies

6 cups Cookie Mix
4 eggs
3 teaspoons vanilla
1 cup peanut butter (the more natural you can find the better!)

Mix all ingredients together. Roll little balls and place them on the cookie sheet. Then take a fork and press down. Bake at 350 for 13 minutes until done.

＊＊＊

There are many books at your local library which have more recipes for you to use regarding home mixes. Mixes save hundreds of dollar per year and they are so simple to make yourself!

Being Frugal With Money

Tips to handle money:

~ Always save your annual tax information for seven years.

~ Try to put aside 1/8 of your paycheck automatically into a higher interest yielding savings account.

~ Try to have two months worth of income saved in case of an emergency.

~   Do not ever be tempted to use a credit card to pay your monthly household payments.

~   Always know how much your household debts are.

~   Try not to use credit cards unless you know you are going to pay them off the following month and are only using them for free air miles. If you can't control your spending, you shouldn't have one at all.

~   Never purchase anything with the thought that you can pay later with credit.

~   Write down how much you spend on frivolous entertainment and pleasures. Keep a budget for entertainment and do not allow yourselves to go over that budget.

Frugal Entertainment for Motherhood

What can you do that doesn't cost a whole lot these days?

Frugal Fun Times With Children:

1) Go to your closest National Park and hike.

2) While hiking teach your children how to make a shelter and other survival skills.

3) Try a picnic outing. Pack all your favorites and head to a cozy picnic spot either by a lake, on a mountain, or just at your favorite city park!

4) Fishing at your local lake or stream.

5) Basketball at the local park.

6) Tennis at the city recreational center for free.

7) Have tea & scones with your girls; cookies and milk with your boys. Make the cookies or scones together.

8) Creation Time. This is a time when all the children gather around together and mother brings out something to create.

9) Have a singing party. It doesn't matter if anyone can keep in tune or not. Send out invitations and plan ahead. Everyone will enjoy it!

10) Go stream watching. Sit down by a stream and just watch what comes floating by. Wade in the shallow parts.

11) Declare a READING CIRCLE! Everyone sits around with a short story. After everyone is finished they pass their book to the right. After each person has read all the books, everyone sits on the book. Each person takes a turn describing the book they are sitting on and others have to guess the title.

11) When it's cold out, grab your family and play two of your favorite games to the bitter end! Don't forget the hot chocolate.

12) Have a family Bible study and discussion. Read an article or a Scripture verse and have each person say what they think it means, or what it means to them.

13) Try Origami. All ages can enjoy creating little things out of the brightly colored paper. It's very inexpensive and you can check out an Origami How-To book at your local library.

14) Try growing a vegetable garden. All it costs you is seeds and a lot of elbow grease. Get everyone involved and this can be a wonderful hobby throughout your whole life. It also saves on food, by the way.

15) Plant a fruit tree and in the future you can make jams, can the fruit and more!

16) Grow herbs. Learn how to season your food with them. Study as a family and see which you like and which you don't!

17) Join a zoo. Meaning, purchase a family membership to your local zoo. It is usually under $40 for a whole year for a family. It is wonderful to take all the children and visit their favorite animal each week. After that initial cost, it is absolutely free. Take a picnic or sack lunch and spend the day!

18) Call your local museum and ask if they offer complimentary visits. Usually, each museum has four days a year in which they offer free entrance rates!

19) Have friends over for a potluck supper. Have a Bible study or play some fun games.

Outings with Hubby:

1) Auctions. Don't laugh! But try going to an auction. Not only are they highly entertaining, they are also a place where a frugal couple can find quality furniture and other things!

2) A moonlight walk around the neighborhood.

3) Cook something together.

4) Cuddle up and discuss a Christian book together.

5) Plan a camping trip.

6) Find a two for one coupon and splurge on dinner.

Music:

1) Volunteer at your local theater. This enables your older children to enjoy musicals and symphonies, that otherwise they might not be able to afford.

2) Borrow music CD's and tapes from your local library instead of purchasing them.

3) Have a radio night where you listen to the radio station of your choice, (we like our local traditional Christian station).

4) Go to your local Goodwill Store or Salvation Army Store. You will be surprised at the instruments people give away. You can find a guitar for under $20 and some people have even been fortunate enough to buy saxophones, flutes, pianos and more for under $100! Spending the initial investment of that instrument is worth all the hours of simple enjoyment later.

5) Check out the "teach yourself" music lessons at your local library.

6) Ask your local home school support group if they have a symphony or band that you may join. If they don't, start one!

Frugality is a way of life. It is choosing to not live above your means and to enjoy the simple things of life. Stop and smell the roses. Look at the stars. Create paper snowflakes. Take great enjoyment in the beautiful things that God has created in His wisdom. He has given us an abundant life here on planet earth. Don't be fooled into thinking that the only way you can enjoy yourself is if you are caught up in the entertainment of the world.

In your notebook, write down fun things that you enjoy doing that do not cost a penny. Remember to keep your notebook where you can always add to it. Frugality is a daily challenge and is such a rewarding way to live!

CHAPTER TWELVE

➥ *Not the End of the Story...* ➥

"She looketh well to the ways of her household, and eateth not the bread of idlenss. Her children arise up, and call her blessed; her husband also, and he praiseth her. Many daughters have done virtuously, but thou excellest them all. Favour is deceitful, and beauty is vain; but a woman that feareth the Lord, she shall be praised. Giver her of the fruit of her hands; and let her own works praise her in the gates." Proverbs 31:27-31

Preparing Your Hope Chest, the book, may seem to have come to a conclusion, but the actual preparation of YOUR hope chest will, oddly enough, never come to an end.

Even after you are married you will find that there are many more skills that you may have overlooked during your training period for being a wife and mother.

In Christ, we will always be perfected until the end, the Scriptures tell us.

Our area of female life, according to the Bible, is in the home. This is why it is so important that young women realize when they are young that they need to truly begin preparing their hope chests now.

They shouldn't wait until they are in their later teen years, right before marriageable age, and then rush to learn these invaluable skills.

Always keep your heart open to sound instruction. Prepare your mind and hands for the work that will be your responsibility when you get married.

Actually Be DOERS, Not Hearers Only

When you take a look at the resources listed at the back of the book, you will find that it may take a whole lifetime to study just the books on frugality! There are millions of ideas out there, but if we spend all of our time reading how to do something rather than getting ready and actually start doing it ourselves, its rather foolish, don't you think?

You will find, and maybe you have already seen this, that there may be a tendency to only learn about things. But in actuality, we never lift a finger. Sometimes that's the way the world teaches. They fill the student's brains with knowledge that is very difficult to apply to every day living.

We must break out of that tendency and start living and being a DOER of the Word of God!

For womankind, that is being a homemaker...

More Ideas

In this book, you have just barely touched the surface of preparation for womanhood. Once you have mastered the beginning skills in this book you might wish to pursue the following:

Gardening - There have been many a young wife who is not able to truly make ends meet with the allowance that her husband gives her. These frugal young ladies have simply gone outside of their rental home, and after asking permission, have dug up a garden area (you can rent a tiller for $15 an hour) and planted seeds and grown most of their fresh vegetables throughout the spring and summer. Gardening is one of the most rewarding occupations. The Scriptures use a lot of gardening and farming parables; and, as you are digging and working with your hands in the soil, it is wonderful to ponder on the Lord's wisdom.

Growing Fruit Trees - Fruit trees do not take that much care, with the exception of the pruning and the training of their branches. But the fruit that they yield is a welcome addition to the families' pantry! How much fun it is to can and make jam from fresh peaches. Apple butter and apple sauce from the apple tree is another real treat.

Hospitality - There are wonderful books written encouraging hospitality. But remember this, true hospitality comes from the heart. It is not the elegant and expensive table or food. It is not the clever or witty conversation. Hospitality is making those who visit your home feel welcome and cared for. Gather ideas for your own company and think of their welfare and comfort as you do so.

Flower Arranging - There is nothing so satisfying as to see a beautiful bouquet which you have picked from your own garden. The arranging is great, but the growing of the arrangement is even better!

Making Baskets - Basket weaving is a fun art to learn. In the olden days, women had to make baskets in order to have places to organize their belongings. They also needed them to help with doing chores and to carry things. Today, it is an art and the baskets are basically for decoration.

Spinning - In our day and age, we don't have to spin our wool in order to knit or crochet. But a hundred years ago that was normal for womankind. You might want to check out one of the Spinning magazines and see if you would like this ancient art.

Stationery - How much fun it is to give and receive homemade cards which are from the heart. There is nothing more enjoyable than to read a hand written poem and see a beautiful picture painted by a loved one. You may also want to try making your own stationery with stamps and ink.

Nursing the elderly & the sick - As you get older, your family members are getting older also. Some day you may be required to care for an aging parent or grandparent.

Health & Nutrition for your Family - This study is a continuous pursuit as finding recipes that appeal to your whole families' taste is sometimes difficult.

Bible Studying - This really should be at the top of the list. As you go about your day, always think about lessons that you are learning in the Lord and then jot them down on a little notebook that you put in the pocket of your dress or apron. Later, when you are having a Bible study with your family, pull this out and discuss what you are learning.

Handling Your Allowance - Budgeting is sometimes difficult. Learn now through library books and experience how to handle money. Some books say to divide your money in three ways, spending, savings and tithe, other books say different things. Find a system that you can handle and learn it now. This way, when you are learning to work with the allowance that your husband will give you, you will be able to manage it well.

Gifts - There is always an occasion when you will need to give gifts. Learn frugal ways to make the most of your money when gift giving. Check out craft books and homemade gift books from the library. There is nothing more well thought of than a clever, hand made gift.

Child Care - Mothers aren't born into this world with the knowledge of how to care for children. There have been mothers who have had their fifth child and yet forget when to start solid food, when to give honey and not too! It is an ongoing learning and relearning process. Start now to study how to care for children so that you won't be overwhelmed in the future when you have your own.

These are just a few topics in which you may want to research further.

We pray that you will be joyful and excited when you think of becoming a wife and mother! Lovingly cherish your hope chest and all of its belonging and what it stands for, and then when you have a little girl of your own someday, you can pass that on to her. Even more, you will have an endless amount of wisdom and knowledge with which to prepare her just as your mother is preparing you!

"See then that ye walk circumspectly, not as fools, but as wise, redeeming the time, because the days are evil. Wherefore be ye not unwise, but understanding what the will of the Lord is."
Ephesians 5:24

RESOURCES

Chapter 4 Handiworks

Craft Yarn Council of America
P.O. Box 9
Gastonia, NC 28053
Tel: 704-824-7838
Fax: 704-824-0630
E-mail: cycainfo@aol.com

Web sites addresses:
www.knitandcrochet.com
www.learntoknit.com
www.learntocrochet.com
www.warmupamerica.com
www.craftyarncouncil.com

ASN Publishing
1415 Linda Vista Dr.
San Marcos, CA 92069
Web site: www.asnpub.com
The American School of Needlework publishes books of instructions and designs for knitting, crocheting, needlework and quilting, which are sold in craft departments and by direct mail.

Acordis Acrylic Fibers
15720 John J. Delaney Dr. Ste 204
Charlotte, NC 28277-2747
Web site: www.courtelle.com
Courtelle is the quality-assured brand from Acordis Acrylic Fibers, the world's leading supplier of dyed acrylic fiber for knitwear and hand-knitting yarns. Equally at home in 100% acrylic form or in blends with natural fibers, and an extensive library of colors, we are one of the world leaders in supplying acrylic fiber for the craft yarn market.

All American Crafts Inc.
243 Newton-Sparta Rd.
Newton, NJ 07860
Web sites: www.knitnstyle.com and www.crochetfantasy.com
Publishers of Knit 'n Style and Crochet Fantasy Magazines, plus a variety of publications for the crafts, wood and paint industries.

Annie's Attic
111 Corporate Dr.

Big Sandy, TX 75755
Web site: www.anniesattic.com
Publishers of needlecraft magazines and books under the Annie's Attic, Needlecraft Shop and
House of White Birches brand names.

Bernat, Lily and Patons Yarns, Inc.

P.O. Box 40
Listowel, OntariCanada N4W 3H3
Web site: www.bernat.com
Spinrite, Inc. manufactures an extensive line of acrylic, blended and natural fiber yarns for the
hand knitting, crocheting and craft yarn markets. It is known for its Bernat (Berella), Lily
(Sugar 'n Cream), and Phentex product lines.

Better Homes and Gardens Crafts Group

1912 Grand Ave.
Des Moines, IA 50309-3379
Web site: www.bhg.com/crafts
Publishers of America's favorite how-to crafts magazines: American Patchwork & Quilting®,
Cross Stitch & Needlework®, Decorative Woodcrafts®, and Crafts & Decorating Showcase™.

Boye Needle/Wrights

South St.
W. Warren, MA 01092
Web site: www.wrights.com
The Boye Needle name is synonymous with a fine line of knitting needles featuring "Perfection
Points," and a full line of crochet hooks with uniquely Boye Tapered Throat design. In addition,
Boye manufactures a full line of knit and crochet accessories and beginners' how-to knit and
crochet books.

Caron International

P.O. Box 200
Washington, NC 27889
Web site: www.caron.com
Caron International yarns and latch hook kits are familiar favorites. Latch hook designs
include: Pooh®, Looney Tunes®, Mickey Unlimited®, NASCAR®, and more. From value-
priced yarn to ultra-soft baby yarns, Caron is known for quality and consistent color. Now, all
Caron yarns are backed by the Good Housekeeping Seal's money-back guarantee.

Cast On Magazine

524 W. 5th Ave., Unit B
Knoxville, TN 37917
Website: http://www.tkga.com
E-mail: tkga@tkga.com
Cast On is the educational journal for knitters and is published five times a year. Regular
features include new product reviews, detailed technique articles, patterns and chapter news. It
is published by The Knitting Guild of America (TKGA), the national organization for knitting
enthusiasts, representing over 12,000 members. TKGA sponsors annual and regional conferences.

Crafts Magazine

Primedia Special Interest Publications
News Plaza
2 News Plaza
Peoria, IL 61656
Web site: www.craftsmag.com
Crafts Magazine is the perfect companion for creating personalized gifts and decorating touches. Published 10 times a year, Crafts is the ultimate source for a wide variety of project ideas. Every issue includes plenty on needlecrafts, including crochet, knitting and embroiderySo comeme join our creative family! To subscribe call: 888.734.9740 or Email: crafts@primediasi.com. For the trade, there is Craftrends Magazine.

Family Circle Easy Knitting

161 Sixth Ave.
New York, NY 10013
Web site: www.vogueknitting.com
From the fashion runways of Europe to baby's nursery, Vogue Knitting Magazine and Family Circle Easy Knitting capture the latest knit and crochet design to please everyone, from the most sophisticated knitter to the beginner. Both magazines are published three times a year and include new products, book reviews and news of interest.

Interweave Knits

201 E. Fourth St.
Loveland, C80537-5655
Web site: www.interweave.com
Interweave Press publishes seven magazines and over a hundred high-quality books about the things we love: fiber, thread, crafts, beads, herbs, natural health, gardening, cooking. Of these seven, five are craft magazines—Interweave Knits, PieceWork, Beadwork, Handwoven and Spin-Off. Of our 55 craft book titles, 24 are focused on knitting.

Krause Publications

700 East State St.
Iola, WI 54990-0001
Web site: www.krause.com
Krause publishes 35 hobby magazines, including Arts & Crafts, Great American Crafts Magazine, Memorymagic, as well as over 500 hardcover books. For the trade, Krause publishes CNA and Craft Supply Magazine.

Lion Brand Yarns

34 W. 15th St.
New York, NY 10011
Web site: www.lionbrand.com
Famous for Quality Since 1878, Lion Brand's popularly priced yarns are known for their unique colors and textures in a variety of weights such as sport (Jamie), knitting worsted (Wool-Ese), chunky (Homespun, Jiffy), and bulky (Chenille Thick & Quick). Labels feature free instructions to make useful and meaningful keepsakes.

Red Heart® Yarns

Two Lakepointe Plaza

4135 So. Stream Blvd
Charlotte, NC 28217
Web site: www.coatsandclark.com
Red Heart® yarns offer consistent quality, value and brilliant colors, including no-dye-lot
solids. For maximum wash performance and a traditional hand, choose Super Saver, Classic,
Sport, Baby Sport, and Baby Fingering. For soft hand and wash performance, try new Soft and
Baby Soft. And for ultimate softness and luster, choose TLC®.

Solutia/Acrilan® Fibers

320 Interstate N. Pkwy. Ste. 500
Atlanta, GA 30339
Web site: www.thesmartyarns.com
Solutia Inc. is the largest producer of acrylic fibers in the United States. Our Acrilan® fiber is
perfect for hand-knit and crocheted designs due to its soft hand and excellent colorfastness. The
popular Bounce-Back® fiber provides unique benefits because they maintain their original
shape wash after wash. Acrilan and Bounce Back fibers make TheSmartYarns.com.

TMA Yarns

206 W. 140th St.
Los Angeles, CA 90061
All TMA Yarns are no-dye-lot acrylic yarns and manufactured in the U.S.A. Our shrink and
stretch resistant, 4-ply worsted weight line includes "Love Knit," "Pop'n," "Fashion Knit,"
"Pioneer," and "Fashion Knit Christmas" and "Victorian Elegance." In 3-ply, we feature "All
Seasons," a sport yarn and for baby, our baby/sport "Softer than Angels," the super-soft
antibacterial yarn.

XRX, Inc.

231 S. Phillips Ave. Ste. 400
Sioux Falls, SD 57104
E-mail: circulation@xrx-inc.com
Web site: www.knittinguniverse.com
Knitter's Magazine, published quarterly by XRX, Inc., is celebrating 15 years and 56 issues
worth of great knits. XRX alsconducts Stitches regional knitting conferences and camps; and
publishes XRX Books, featuring authors such as Sally Melville, Jean Moss, Meg Swansen, and
Anna Zilboorg. XRX maintains a comprehensive knitting web site at
www.knittinguniverse.com.

Chapter 6

National Academy of Needle Arts
P.O. Box 17655 * Anaheim Hills, CA   92817 * 714-998-7644

The American Sewing Guild:

Chapters of the **American Sewing Guild** typically cover geographic areas ranging from 50 to
75 miles in radius.
Many chapters contain Neighborhood Groups which meet at various times to accommodate the
needs of local members. If you want information about a specific chapter and its Neighborhood
Groups, please contact the Chapter President listed.

If no chapter exists near you and you feel that there is sufficient group interest to form one, please contact the Association headquarters for guidelines on starting a Chapter of **ASG.**

The state chapters are listed below:
Contact 816 444-3500 for more information

ALABAMA
Birmingham Chapter ASG
Mildred Mathews
3472 Chapel Ln
Birmingham, AL 35226
(205) 823-7957
sewmmat@aol.com

ALASKA
Eagle River Chapter
Vicki Portwood
8315 Eleusis Dr
Anchorage, AK 99502
(907) 243-7697
portwood@alaska.net

ARIZONA
Phoenix Chapter ASG
Marjorie Boydston
1416 E. Westchester Dr.
Tempe, AZ 85283-3163
(480) 491-9481
mboydstonasg@worldnett.att.net
Prescott Chapter ASG
Pat Sherman
PO Box 25038
Prescott Valley, AZ 86312
(520) 772-8418
Tucson Chapter ASG
Catherine Biggers
2371 N. Lake Star Dr.
Tucson, AZ 85749-8709
(520) 749-3957
cmbiggers@uswest.net
Yuma Chapter ASG
Toni A. Seward
8891 S. 48th Ave.
Yuma, AZ 85364
(520) 782-5529
toniseward@icqmail.com

ARKANSAS
Sorry, there are no established chapters in Arkansas yet.

CALIFORNIA
Bakersfield Chapter ASG
Donna Stauffer
3604 Prestige Ln
Bakersfield, CA 93313
(661) 837-2664
Monterey Chapter ASG
Pat James
521 Knoll Ln
Aromas, CA 95004
(831) 726-3016
toolpouch@gowebway.com
Orange County Chapter ASG
Ann Beale
P.O. Box 1294
Newport Beach, CA 92659-1294
(949) 650-7397
Riverside/San Bernardino Chapter
Geneva Noble
10820 Holmes Ave.
Mira Loma, CA 91752-2653
(909) 371-7239
asg@urs2.net

Sacramento Chapter ASG
Jeanette Redding
4619 Las Lindas Way
Carmichael, CA 95608-1509
(916) 962-1396
netty@pacbell.net

San Diego Chapter ASG
Kathy White
6710 Barberry Pl
Carlsbad, CA 92009
(760) 603-0242
KathyWht@aol.com
San Jose Chapter ASG
Patricia "Pat" Moore
352 King Drive
South San Francisco, CA 94080-3036
(650) 588-6488
NLM6141@aol.com
Santa Rosa Chapter ASG
Carol Jacobsen
2525 Laguna Vista Dr.

Novato, CA 94945-1562
(415) 892-1834
Visalia Chapter ASG
Connie Wong
3133 S Avocado St
Visalia, CA 93277
(559) 734-3231
cwong23@hotmail.com
Walnut Creek Chapter ASG
Janice N Harski
PO Box 5948
Concord, CA 94524-0948
(925) 942-3372
(925) 942-3353 fax
wlntcrkasg@yahoo.com

COLORADO
Denver Chapter ASG
Rebecca Pressley
P.O. Box 745759
Arvada, CO 80006-5759
(303) 494-0861
rebeccasew@worldnet.att.net
Ft. Collins Chapter ASG
Marjorie R. Clark
1305 Skyline Dr.
Ft. Collins, CO 80521-4313
(970) 484-0347
Greeley Chapter ASG
Fern Wright
2544 14th Ave Ct
Greeley, CO 80631-8321
(970) 352-8571

CONNECTICUT
Danbury Chapter ASG
Anna Mazur
48 Knollwood Ln
Avon, CT 06001-2701
(860) 678-0905
MazCouture@aol.com

MASSACHUSETTS
Boston Chapter ASG
Ellen V. Paulsen
334 Brickett Hill Rd
Pembroke, NH 03275
(603) 224-2266
evpaulsen@aol.com
Springfield Chapter ASG

Pauline E. Mulak
111 Lachine Street
Chicopee, MA 01020-3331
(413) 594-4183
Pokerchp77@aol.com
RHODE ISLAND
**Sorry, there are no established chapters
in Rhode Island yet.**

FLORIDA
Ft. Lauderdale Chapter ASG
Leilani Miller
21375 Sonesta Way
Boca Raton, FL 33433-2303
(561) 488-2026
lanisews@juno.com
Ft. Myers Chapter ASG
Marlene Boling-Libner
P.O. Box 338
Ft. Myers, FL 33902-0338
(941) 337-7021
clasylyn@gate.com
Jacksonville Chapter ASG
Sandy Ingersoll
1129 Fromage Circle E
Jacksonville, FL 32225
(904) 720-0018
Sandrasews2@aol.com

Miami Chapter ASG
Rose Blitz
15152 SW 95th Lane
Miami, FL 33196
(305) 385-7760
KBLITZ9553@aol.com

Ocala Chapter
Pam McIntyre
10204 SW 55th Ln
Gainesville, FL 32608
(352) 375-3103
mcpam@aol.com

Orlando Chapter ASG
Carolyn Haight
7029 Carlene Drive
Plainfield, IN 46168-1171
(317) 837-9029
esme@iquest.net
Kokomo Chapter ASG
Pat Skillington

Orlando, FL 32835-1803
(407) 298-2398
Cherjens@aol.com
Sarasota Chapter ASG
Carroll Jenkins
4634 McIntosh Rd
Sarasota, FL 34233-1931
(941) 922-6300
cmj-asg@home.com
Tampa Chapter ASG
Melanie Toppe
210 14th Ave N
St. Petersburg, FL 33701-1128
(727) 823-1220
mtoppezz@aol.com
Titusville Chapter ASG
Kathy Matura
588 Gardenia Cir
Titusville, FL 32796-2443
(407) 383-1292
sewfun@ham.net

GEORGIA

Atlanta Chapter ASG
Myla D. Chapman
1204 Pineglen Dr.
Riverdale, GA 30296-3226
(770) 997-0186
ASGATLANTA@aol.com

Macon Chapter ASG
Wanda Hamrick
100 Hilltop Cir.
Macon, GA 31210-9701
(912) 994-0225
chamrick@mindspring.com

HAWAII
Honolulu Chapter ASG
Shelly Caldwell
For contact information for the Hawaii chapter, please
call or e-mail ASG Headquarters.

IDAHO
Boise Chapter ASG
Eileen Givens
4411 S. Mustang Dr.
Boise, ID 83709-5018

(208) 362-0257
egivens@idahopower.com

ILLINOIS
Chicago Chapter ASG
Aileen Vogel
510 N Worth Ave
Elgin, IL 60123-3453
(847) 742-1470
AVogelsew@aol.com
Peoria Chapter ASG
Marjorie E. York
P.O. Box 6102
Peoria, IL 61601-6102
(309) 692-2735
lmyork@horizon222.net
Springfield Chapter ASG
Sarah Brogdon
2535 Rees Rd
Franklin, IL 62638
(217) 675-2060

INDIANA
Evansville Chapter ASG
Evelyn L. MaVeety
1931 Eastland Dr.
Evansville, IN 47715-6169
(812) 473-5356
elmaveet@evansville.net
Ft. Wayne Chapter ASG
Marcy O'Laughlin
8325 Calera Dr.
Ft. Wayne, IN 46818-1893
(219) 489-5045
Huntingburg Chapter ASG
Shirley Biehl
PO Box 35
Dale, IN 47523-9802
(812) 683-4455
ssssb@webtx.net
Indianapolis Chapter ASG
Robin Elizabeth Parsley
163 N. West St.

5 Lakeview Dr
Greentown, IN 46936
(765) 628-2281
lake5skilli@juno.com

Marion Chapter ASG
Janet Fedor
1509 W Overlook Rd.
Marion, IN 46952-1124
(765) 662-8981
mf1509@yahoo.com

Richmond Chapter ASG
Georgia Lyons
3256 Straightline Pike
Richmond, IN 47374-7262
(765) 935-5748

IOWA
Ames Chapter ASG
Marilyn Stenberg
1907 Polk Dr.
Ames, IA 50010-4314
(515) 232-0435
mstenberg@ames.net

Cedar Rapids Chapter ASG
Beth Riherd
3004 Huxley Lane SW
Cedar Rapids, IA 52404
(319) 396-4557

Waterloo Chapter ASG
Pat McKinney
2148 150th Street
Traer, IA 50675-9566
(319) 478-2194

KANSAS
Flint Hills Chapter ASG
Velma Walker
545 Road 140
Emporia, KS 66801-7530
(316) 342-4091

Pittsburg Chapter ASG
Joy Holloway
112 E. Saint John Street
Girard, KS 66743-1341
(316) 724-4473

Wichita Chapter ASG
Denise Dias
17000 W Maple 5-E

Goddard, KS 67052
(316) 794-2533
Fax (316) 722-7727
ddias@oz.oznet.ksu.edu

KENTUCKY
Owensboro Chapter ASG
Donna M. Stuerzenberger
3400 Hummingbird Loop S
Owensboro, KY 42301
(270) 926-2885

LOUISIANA
Baton Rouge Chapter ASG
Pie Michelli
15442 Patricia Dale Dr
Baton Rouge, LA 70819
(225) 272-1087
michelli@premier.net

Many Chapter ASG
Kelly Pearson
2542 Zachary Taylor Rd
Many, LA 71449
(318) 256-2532
midnightsewin@hotmail.com

MAINE
Bangor Chapter ASG
Debbie Lancaster
3 Spring St
Bucksport, ME 04416-4013
(207) 469-1059
MSL620@aol.com

NEW HAMPSHIRE
Sorry, there are no established chapters in New Hampshire.

VERMONT
Sorry, there are no established chapters in Vermont.

MARYLAND
Bowie Chapter ASG
Jeanne Perrone
13600 Hopkins Rd
Germantown, MD 20874-1401
(301) 528-8935

(301) 903-3960 fax
jeannesews@juno.com

MICHIGAN

For Detorit, MI chapter information please contact the ASG Headquarters.

Grand Rapids Chapter ASG
Melody Shryock
5003 Boyd Ave NE
Grand Rapids, MI 49525
(616) 361-6697
mkshryock@juno.com
Kalamazoo Chapter ASG
Janet Dapson
6951 East AB Ave
Richland, MI 49083
(616) 964-6450
email@anatechltdusa.com
Lansing Chapter ASG
Judy Huhn
8650 W. Centerline Rd.
St. Johns, MI 48879
(517) 224-3518
djhuhn@voyager.net

MINNESOTA
Duluth Chapter ASG
Carol Grossman
RR 1, Box 71B
Tamarack, MN 55787
(218) 768-3619
Minneapolis/St. Paul Chapter ASG
LaVerne Bell
P.O. Box 21214
Minneapolis, MN 55421-0214
(612) 789-1734

MISSISSIPPI
Sorry, there are no established chapters in Mississippi yet.

TENNESSEE
Sorry, there are no established chapters in Tennessee yet.

MISSOURI

Kansas City Chapter ASG
Amy Marlo
10232 Outlook Dr.
Overland Park, KS 66207-3019
(913) 649-9661
ajm@americancentury.com
St. Louis Chapter ASG
Nancy Seibert
424 Belleview Ave
St. Louis, MO 63119
(314) 374-7397
nancyseibert@yahoo.com

MONTANA
Sidney Chapter ASG
Mavis Berry
HC 2 Box 2
Cartwright, ND 58838-9703
(701) 744-5112

NEBRASKA
Omaha Chapter ASG
Janice Sedivy
PO Box 706
Valley, NE 68064-0706
(402) 359-2302

NEVADA
Las Vegas Chapter ASG
Bobbie Litzinger
10112 Plomosa Pl.
Las Vegas, NV 89134-6900
(702) 255-6303
Northern Nevada Chapter ASG
Rosalie Pelham
8000 Blackfoot Way
Reno, NV 89506
(775) 972-6213
NorthernNevadaASG@juno.com

NEW JERSEY
Clifton/North New Jersey Chapter ASG
Sara Ann Megletti
273 Andover-Sparta Rd.
Newton, NJ 07860-6101
(973) 729-2774
marasim@compuserve.com
Princeton Chapter ASG
Mary Lou Giacomelli

PO Box 356
Mount Laurel, NJ 08054-0356
(609) 953-9059
bobandmarylou@compuserve.com
Union/Central New Jersey Chapter
Judy Butler
454 North Ave
Fanwood, NJ 07023-1321
(908) 889-0750
Judy_Butler@worldnet.att.net

NEW YORK
Albany Chapter ASG
Eleanor G. Holbein
382 Sweetman Rd.
Ballston Spa, NY 12020-3107
(518) 882-6157
Buffalo Chapter ASG
Kim Cardina
214 Brinton St
Buffalo, NY 14216
(716) 836-5279
NY/Nassau/QueensChapter ASG
Heather See
84 Long Dr
Hempstead, NY 11550-4708
(516) 481-2365
hsee@seefactor.com
Rochester Chapter ASG
Linda Ims
926 Little Pond Way
Webster, NY 14580-8920
(716) 671-1101
Syracuse Chapter ASG
Susan Bray
2408 Sourwood Dr
Phoenix, NY 13135-9519
(315) 695-4564
suebray@twcny.rr.com

NEW MEXICO
Albuquerque Chapter ASG
Nancy Flanagan
PO Box 14592
Albuquerque, NM 87191-4592
(505) 839-4370
trix@flash.net
Las Cruces Chapter ASG
Mary Tiffany
PO Box 1656

Las Cruces, NM 88004
(505) 532-1740
matiffany@aol.com

NORTH CAROLINA
Charlotte Chapter ASG
Barbara "Bobbie" Bullard
6511 Buggy Whip Lane
Waxhaw, NC 28173-9789
(704) 843-1424
bullards@earthlink.net
Raleigh Chapter ASG
Peg Henderson
6221 Sweden Dr
Raleigh, NC 27612
(919) 781-6106
sewhenderson@aol.com

SOUTH CAROLINA
Sorry, there are no established chapters in South Carolina yet.

NORTH DAKOTA
Bismarck Chapter ASG
Marie Gabel
5861 48th Ave. SE
Bismarck, ND 58504
(701) 258-3723

OHIO
Akron/Canton Chapter ASG
Rose Marie Houser
6945 Rolling Ridge NE
North Canton, OH 44721-3060
(330) 492-0716
rhouser@ezo.net
Cincinnati Chapter ASG
Dee Atkinson
P.O. Box 15874
Cincinnati, OH 45215-0874
(513) 821-4287
dee_asg@patternstudio.com
Cleveland Chapter ASG
Jan Nyegard
309 Water St
Chardon, OH 44024
(440) 285-7296
sewforsure@core.com
Columbus Chapter ASG
Michele McIntosh

4012 Sandy Ridge Dr
Columbus, OH 43204
(614) 275-4845
stitchedblessings@hotmail.com
Niles Chapter ASG
Susan Stoddart
14755 Robinson Rd
Newton Falls, OH 44444-9607
(330) 538-3182
institches5848@aol.com
North Olmsted Chapter ASG
Elaine A. Boerke
7307 Hacienda Dr
Parma, OH 44130-5236
(440) 842-2388
EABASGNO@aol.com

OKLAHOMA
Oklahoma City Chapter ASG
Dawn Andrew
8505 N Eastern
Oklahoma City, OK 73131
(405) 478-0409
dwnandrew@aol.com
Tulsa Chapter ASG
Maj Smith
2633 E. 38th St.
Tulsa, OK 74105-8206
(918)743-0815
majcouture@aol.com

OREGON
Medford Chapter ASG
Karen Rethman-Foll
925 "B" St
Ashland, OR 97520-2031
(541) 482-3544
krf@mind.net
Portland Chapter ASG
Joyce Wold
12923 SW Laurmont Dr.
Tigard, OR 97223-1675
(503) 524-5400
mwold@teleport.com
Salem Chapter ASG
Phyllis Prysock
853 Creekside Dr SE
Salem, OR 97306-1755

(503) 540-3162
dandpprysock@prodigy.net
PENNSYLVANIA
Philadelphia Chapter ASG
Carol Ragin
8535 Thouron Ave
Philadelphia, PA 19150
(215) 242-2898
crseamer@aol.com
Pittsburgh Chapter ASG
Janet Staats
130 Carpenter Ln.
N. Huntingdon, PA 15642-1277
(724) 863-7555
jshjdh@ckt.net
Scranton Chapter ASG
Millicent Erickson
517 Gladiola Dr.
Clarks Summit, PA 18411-2115
(717) 586-5798
State College Chapter ASG
Mary McMonagle
PO Box 0008
Lemont, PA 16851-0008
(814) 692-5393
m3sews@earthlink.net

SOUTH DAKOTA
Sorry, there are no established chapters in South Dakota yet.

TEXAS
Abilene Chapter ASG
Antoinette Brown
PO Box 1677
Abilene, TX 79604
(915) 795-9302
otjazz@worldnet.att.net

Corpus Christi Chapter ASG
Sarah Pitzer
6417 Longmeadow
Corpus Christi, TX 78413-2702
(361) 991-7174
pitzoo@corpus.quik.com
Dallas/Ft. Worth Chapter ASG
Carole Carter

315 Ashley Dr
Coppell, TX 75019-3265
Carole_Carter@hotmail.com

Houston Chapter ASG
Darlene Jackson
14602 Forest Lodge Dr
Houston, TX 77070-2239
(713) 867-9186
asg@houston.rr.com

San Antonio Chapter ASG
Debra Lally
603 Amistad
Universal City, TX 78148
(210) 658-8220
djlall@aol.com

Wichita Falls Chapter ASG
Joan Schaffner
2107 E Crafton
Henrietta, TX 76365
(940) 538-5057
sewnsew@wf.quik.com

UTAH

Salt Lake City Chapter ASG
Sandra Jones
4674 S. Danna Cir.
Salt Lake City, UT 84119-6007
(801) 966-0355
deckjone@slkc.uswest.net

DELAWARE
Sorry, there are no established chapters in Delaware yet.

VIRGI
NIA

Hampton Roads Chapter ASG
Nancy Powers
1121 Rockbridge Avenue
Norfolk, VA 23508-1417
(757) 423-7088
npowers@dollartree.com

Radford Chapter ASG
Edith Carter
Radford University
Box 6924
Radford, VA 24142-6924

(540) 831-5510
ecarter@runet.edu
Richmond Chapter ASG
Maureen Heck
3410 Northridge Rd
Richmond, VA 23235-1350
(804) 320-5563
MJHECK@mediaone.net
Roanoke Chapter ASG
Susan Brown
3448 Harbor Wood Road
Salem, VA 24153-5732
(540) 389-3245

WASHINGTON DC
Sorry, there are no established chapters in Washington DC yet.

WEST VIRGINIA
Sorry, there are no established chapters in West Virginia yet.

WASHINGTON

Bellevue Chapter ASG
Shelley Clark
bellevueasg@gtemail.net

Olympia Chapter ASG
Sandra Cagle
6011 Winnwood Drive S.E.
Olympia, WA 98513
(360) 456-8509
asgwa@aol.com

Silverdale Chapter ASG
Amanda Beitzel
P.O. Box 2762
Silverdale, WA 98383-2762
(360) 681-0510
beitzels@olympus.net

WISCONSIN
Milwaukee Chapter ASG
Barbara Gambrell
1816 W Grange Ave
Milwaukee, WI 53221
(414) 282-4935

Bski113@aol.com

WYOMING
Laramie Chapter ASG
Maryjo Downey
PO Box 1555
Laramie, WY 82073
(307) 745-8159
manganent@aol.com

Chapter 7 Decorating

The Stencil Shoppe, Inc.
2503 Silverside Road
Wilmington, DE 19810
Phone: 302-475-7975
Toll Free: 1-800-822-STEN (7836)

Chapter 8 Kitchen Preparation

The following supplier sells both aluminum, stainless steel and copper pans. Be careful and ask them which items contain aluminum. We liked their resources and they carry a wide variety of household items.

COOKSOURCE, Inc.
P. O. Box 5571
Cary, NC 27511
919.859.3429
919.851.8391 (f)
http://store.yahoo.com/cooksourcestore/info.html

Chapter 9 Cooking

Once-A-Month Cooking : A Proven System for Spending Less Time in the Kitchen and Enjoying Delicious, Homemade Meals Everyday
by Marilyn S. Wilson

Frozen Assets : How to Cook for a Day and Eat for a Month
by Deborah Taylor-Hough

 Available from Amazon.com

Chapter 11 Frugality

FREE COUPONS on the web. Go to: www.coupons.com You can print out your own grocery coupons from the web sight.

www.thefrugallife.com
www.allthingsfrugal.com
www.miserlymoms.com

www.brightok.net/~neilmayo/ Julie's Frugal Tips: "For those new to this page, it's devoted to my wife who can squeeze pennies out of rocks. Our goal is to present ideas here that are a little bit more than just simple things like saving cans. We're hoping to find things to supplement those basic ideas. . . . By the way, why do hot dogs come in packs of 10 and buns only 8? . . . Wow, for a quirky little home page it surprised me that we made the NSCA WHAT'S NEW TOP 5 LIST the other day. I guess everyone has a little tightwad in 'em." Many links available from this page.

Cheapskate Monthly is a 12-page newsletter that is now available in two formats: a **US-Mail Version** that is delivered to your home every month by the U.S. mail, and the **new Web Version** which is uploaded monthly to the members only section of the CM web site.

The cost to subscribe to either version is currently $18 for one year, or $34 for two years. If you would like to subscribe to both versions simultaneously, you can now do so at the discounted rate of just $30 for one year.

So just think, for less than the cost of a large pizza with everything on it, you can have a full year of unlimited access! And if you're still not sure whether or not you should subscribe, we've even set up a savings calculator to help you see what subscribing to *Cheapskate Monthly* can mean to your financial future.

You may order your subscription in any one of the following ways:

1. By e-mail to: orders@cheapskatemonthly.com

2. By telephone at: 800-550-3502 (Orders only, please!)

3. By mail to:

Cheapskate Monthly Online
    P.O. Box 2076
    Paramount, CA 90723.

The Frugal Gazette!

This newsletter is dedicated to help it's readers reduce the high cost of living. We will help you to examine various expenses in your life and offer suggestions to help you live within your means and allow you to save money for any purpose you see fit

This newsletter is for people at the various extremes of frugality. Perhaps you have the time to pinch every penny and live life as the ultimate tightwad. Great! You will find helpful suggestions to further your quest. If, on the other hand, you have limited time to clip coupons and live such a hectic life that you barely know your kid's names, you too should find some helpful hints to help you feel more in control of your money. Perhaps we will be able to offer suggestions to open your mind to a different way of doing things

Forced Frugality

Many families are being forced to scale back their expenses due to corporate downsizing, layoffs and reorganization. Job security is no longer a benefit offered in the work place. It is shocking to think that nearly 440,000 people were laid-off in 1995 and the trend doesn't seem to be slowing down. In the late 1980's only one out of every three Americans were concerned about losing their jobs or taking a pay cut. Yet, in the mid 1990's, more than half are anxious about job and pay security.

Credit card debt, huge mortgages and living beyond ones means has forced many to re-evaluate their current standard of living and look for alternative methods to reduce expenses. For some, living frugally may have been a choice in the past, but it has now become a necessity.

You are not alone!

Americans now have a total outstanding credit debt of more than $1 trillion. This is a 29 % increase from 1993 levels! Unfortunately, credit card debt increased four to five times faster than income levels over the same period of time. Obviously, we are spending money we do not have.

Voluntary simplicity:

Some people are of the opinion, "don't we have enough already"? This new movement called voluntary simplicity may represent a philosophical shift in thinking or just a survival method. Over consumption is viewed by many as wasteful, harmful, unnecessary and unfulfilling. The stigma once associated with buying used things seems to have changed. Today, if you purchase used items you're viewed as being economical, ecological and smart. Used items are now called "collectibles" or "vintage.

Our goal:

In deciding to live frugally, you will have choices when previously you thought you had none. Cutting back does not have to be painful. However, it does require some thought, planning and education.

The Frugal Gazette is dedicated to providing information and encouragement to successfully pursue frugality. You will be supported in your cost saving goals as you read about the experiences of other readers. The Frugal Gazette will provide an avenue to share your ideas. We always welcome your comments, suggestions and experiences.

The Frugal Gazette
P.O. Box 3395
Newtown, Connecticut 06470-3395
www.frugalgazette.com

Other Resources:

Better Than Store-Bought: A Cookbook by Helen Witty & Elizabeth Colchie, 1985. Out of print.

Cheaper & Better Homemade Alternatives to Store Bought Goods by Nancy Birnes. Shadow Lawn Press, Inc. 1987.

Compleat I Hate to Cook Book by Peg Bracken, paperback, Bantam, 1988. Out of print.

Cooking With the Sun: How to Build and Use Solar Cookers by Beth Halacy, Dan Halacy, paperback, 114 pp., Morning Sun Press, 1992.

Crowned With Silver - Godly Homemaking Magazine, P.O. Box 6338, Longmont, CO 80501

Desperation Dinners! by Beverly Mills and Alicia Ross, paperback, 256 pp., Workman Publishing Co., 1997.

Eat Healthy for $50 a Week: Feed Your Family Nutritious, Delicious Meals for Less by Rhonda Barfield, paperback, 223 pp., Kensington Publishing Corp., 1996.

Frozen Assets: How to Cook for a Day and Eat for a Month by Deborah Taylor-Hough, Champion Press 1998.

Heaven's Flame: A Guide to Solar Cookers by Joe Radabaugh. The author writes that this book seeks to educate the reader on how solar cooking works, so that the reader may cook her own favorite foods using solar heat.

Make Your Own Convenience Foods: How to Make Chemical-Free Foods That Are Fast, Simple, and Economical by Don & Joan German, MacMillan Pub., 1979. Out of print.

Make Your Own Groceries by Daphne Metaxas Hartwig. Bobbs-Merrill Co., Inc., 1979. *More Make Your Own Groceries*, same author, 1983. Both out of print.

Making Food Storage Fun, Fast & Easy by LauraAnne Logar. Available from her right here online. LauraAnne Logar $9 PPD. Or send Money Order for $9 to her at Morgan Hill, CA 95037-6621.

More-With-Less Cookbook by Doris Janzen Longacre and Mary Showalter, paperback, 323 pp., Herald Press, 1976.

Never Throw Out a Banana Again: And 364 Other Ways to Save Money at Home Without Knocking Yourself Out by Darcie Sanders & Martha Bullen, paperback, 168 pp., Crown Publishing, 1995.

Once a Month Cooking: A Time-Saving, Budget-Stretching Plan to Prepare Delicious Meals by Mimi Wilson and Mary Beth Lagerborg, paperback, Focus on the Family, 1994.

Putting Food By by Janet Greene, Ruth Hertzberg, Beatrice Vaughan, 4th ed., paperback, Penguin USA, 1992.

Recipes for a Small Planet by Ellen Buchman Ewald, paperback, Ballentine Books, 1983.

Root Cellaring: Natural Cold Storage of Fruits and Vegetables by Mike Bubel and Nancy Bubel, 2nd ed., paperback, 320 pp., Storey Books, 1991.

Simple Food for the Good Life, Helen Nearing, paperback, Stillpoint Publishing, 1995.

Solar Cooking: A Primer/Cookbook by Harriet Kofalk, paperback, 96 pp., Book Publishing Co., 1997.

Solar Cooking Naturally by Virginia Gurley, 3rd edition, paperback, SunLightWorks, Inc., 1995.

Stocking Up III: The All-New Edition of America's Classic Preserving Guide by Carol Hupping, 3rd ed., hardcover, 627 pp., Rodale Books, 1986.

Stories and Recipes from the Great Depression of the 1930's and More from Your Kitchen in the 80's by Rita Van Amber, paperback, Van Amber Publications, 1986.

The $30 A Week Grocery Budget by Donna McKenna, PO Box 391, Brooklet, GA 30415. Volume #1 $5 ppd. Volume #2 $4.50 ppd. These books may only be purchased directly from the author.

The Use-It-Up Cookbook by Lois Carlson Willand. Ms. Willand writes: "For your information, folks who want to order *The Use-It-Up Cookbook* can have it special ordered by their local bookstore or can order direct from me. The cost is $12.95 postpaid. Send check to Practical Cookbooks, 145 Malcolm Ave. S.E., Minneapolis, MN 55414. 612-378-9697."

Adventures in Simple Living: A Creation-Centered Spirituality by Rich Heffern. Out of print.

Best of The Cheapskate Monthly: Simple Tips for Living Lean in the 90's by Mary Hunt, paperback, 201 pp., St. Martin Mass Market Paperbacks, 1993.

Cheap Tricks (100s of Ways You Can Save 1000s of Dollars!) by Andy Dappen. 1992; 405 pp. ISBN 0-9632577-0-6 $13.95 ($15 postpaid) from Brier Books, PO Box 180, Mountlake Terrace, Seattle, WA 98043; 800/356-9315.

Cheaper & Better Homemade Alternatives to Store Bought Goods by Nancy Birnes. Shadow Lawn Press, Inc. 1987. Out of print.

The Cheapskate Monthly Money Makeover by Mary Hunt, paperback, 209 pp., St. Martin's Mass Market Paperbacks, 1995.

Choose to Reuse: An Encyclopedia of Services, Businesses, Tools & Charitable Programs That Facilitate Reuse by Nikki and David Goldbeck, paperback, 455 pp., Ceres Press, 1995.

Circle of Simplicity: Return to the Good Life, Cecile Andrews, paperback, 288 pp., Harpercollins, 1998.

Country Self-Sufficiency, Pete Mickelson. "*Country Self-Sufficency* describes how to find and build a homestead, complete with garden, greenhouse, crops and animals for all of North America. Chapters include homeschooling, selecting a homestead and living off nature."

Cut Your Bills in Half: Thousands of Tips to Save Thousands of Dollars, Rodale Press. Out of print.

Downwardly Mobile for Conscience Sake, a collection of essays by 10 authors, Dorothy Andersen ed., paperback, Tom Paine Institute, 1995.

The Frugal Mind: 1,483 Money Saving Tips for Surviving the New Millennium by Charlotte Gorman. Nottingham Books, 1998. $19.95. ISBN 0-9625856-2-9.

Getting a Life: Real Lives Transformed by Your Money or Your Life by Jacqueline Blix, David Heitmiller, and Joe Dominguez, hardcover, 364 pp., Viking Press, 1997.

The Good Life: Helen and Scott Nearing's Sixty Years of Self-Sufficient Living, by Helen and Scott Nearing, paperback, 411 pp., Schocken Books, 1990.

High Finance on a Low Budget: Build Wealth Regardless of Your Income, Mark Skousen and Jo Ann Skousen, hardcover, Dearborn Trade, 1992.

How Much Is Enough?: The Consumer Society and the Future of the Earth (The Worldwatch Environmental Alert Series) by Alan Durning, paperback, 200 pp., W. W. Norton, 1992.

How to Get What You Want in Life With the Money You Already Have by Carol Keeffe, paperback, 235 pp., Little Brown, 1995.

How To Live Cheap But Good by Martin Poriss, 1971. Out of print.

How to Live on Almost Nothing and Have Plenty : A Practical Introduction to Small-Scale Sufficient Living by Janet Chadwick. For beginning homesteaders. Out of print.

How to Live on Nothing by Joan Ranson Shortney, 1971. Out of print.

How to Live Rich When You're Not by Rebecca Greer, paperback, Ballantine Books, 1971.

How to Survive Without a Salary: Coping in Today's Inflationary Times by Learning How to Live the Conserver Lifestyle by Charles Long. — New York: Sterling Pub., c1981. — ISBN 0-919157-05X

How to Want What You Have: Discovering the Magic and Grandeur of Ordinary Existence by Timothy Miller, Ph.D., paperback, Avon Books, 1995. ckuter@ix.netcom.com writes: "I just started reading *How to Want What You Have* by Timothy Miller. This is an interesting book about accepting, and recognizing, the blessings that you already have. It points out that the pursuit for More causes many problems. It seems to provide a better focus for the frugal life style."

Living Cheap: Survival Guide to the 1990s by Larry Roth, paperback, Ropubco, 1990. Also *Living Cheap News: The First Two Years*, paperback, 1994, same author and publisher.

Living More With Less by Doris Janzen Longacre, paperback, 294 pp., Herald Press, 1980. This book is on Herald Press's <u>all-time bestseller list</u>, from which you can access their home page and ordering information. Herald Press publishes Mennonite and Anabaptist readings. The Mennonite church seems to have an approach to Christianity that is highly compatible with frugal living, and it has other pages on the Web.

Living Cheaply With Style by Ernest Callenbach. Callenbach is also the author of *Ecotopia*, which is listed in the <u>visions</u> section. *Living Cheaply With Style* can be ordered online from <u>Ronin Books</u>.

Living on a Shoestring: A Survival Guide for Coping With Finances, Furnishings, Recipes, Rents, and Roommates, Etc. by Mike Edelhart, 1980. Out of print.

Living Well on Practically Nothing by Edward Romney, Paladin Press, 1992.

Mark Skousen's 30 Day Plan To Financial Independence: 1001 Ways to Cut Your Expenses by Mark Skousen.

Miserly Moms: Living On One Income In A Two Economy (2nd edition), by Jonni McCoy, $9.99, Full Quart Press, 1996.

The *Mother Earth News Guide to Self-Reliant City Living*, Mother Earth News, 1992. Sections on gardening, energy, transportation, food, livestock, health, home business and community.

Muddling Toward Frugality by Warren Johnson, paperback, Random House, 1977. Out of print. New editioon scheduled for publication this year .

The Penny Pincher's Almanac: Handbook for Modern Frugality by Dean King, Fireside, 1993. *Penny Pinching* by Lee and Barbara Simmons, 4th ed., paperback, Bantam Books, 1997.

A Place Called Simplicity: The Quiet Beauty of Simple Living by Claire Cloninger, paperback, 209 pp., Harvest House, 1993.

Plain and Simple: A Woman's Journey to the Amish by Sue Bender, paperback, 176 pp., Harper San Francisco, 1991.

Saving Money Any Way You Can by Mike Yorkey.

Simple Abundance: A Daybook of Comfort & Joy by Sarah Ban Breathnach ISBN 0-446-51913-8 (hardcover), Warner Books, 1995.

Simple Living by Frank Levering & Wanda Urbanska, paperback, Penguin USA, 1993.

The Simple Living Guide: A Sourcebook for Less Stressful, More Joyful Living by Janet Luhrs, paperback, 352 pp., Broadway Books, 1997.

Simplicity: Notes, Stories and Exercises for Developing Unimaginable Wealth by Mark Burch, paperback, New Society, 1995.

Simplify Your Life: 100 Ways to Slow Down and Enjoy the Things That Really Matter by Elaine St. James ISBN 7868-8000-7.

Small Is Beautiful, E. F. Schumacher, Harper & Row, 1975. Profound ruminations on why our culture is on a path divergent from our spiritual needs, and what might be done to set it right. Schumacher, an economist, sees the discipline of economics as a major source of the errors, and provides thoughtful and extremely well-written explanations and criticisms.

Smart Cents: Creative Tips and Quips for Living the Skinflint Way by Ron and Melodie Moore. Out of print.

The Tightwad Gazette I, II, and III by Amy Dacyczyn, 1993/95/97, Random House. Collected issues of the well-known newsletter on cutting expenses.

This Place on Earth: Home and the Practice of Permanence by Alan Thein Durning, paperback, 336 pp., Sasquatch Books, 1997.

Voluntary Simplicity: Toward a Way of Life That Is Outwardly Simple, Inwardly Rich, Duane

Elgin, paperback, Quill, 1993.

The Wealthy Procrastinator by Henry Cimmer, 1993.

When Money Is the Drug, Donna Boundy, paperback, Harper Collins, 1994: dbl@gozer.osf.org writes: "I'm in the middle of reading *When Money Is the Drug*, which has very interesting things to say about how we deal with money, both as individuals and in this (American) society. It's helped me examine my own mixed feelings about the subject of money. The author does have some useful advice on when it is healthy to *spend* money."

Working Harder Isn't Working: How We Can Save the Environment, the Economy, and Our Sanity by Working Less and Enjoying Life More by Bruce O'Hara, New Star Books, 1993.

The Backyard Homestead Mini-Farm & Garden Log Book by John Jeavons, J. Mogador Griffin & Robin Leler, 1983, Ten Speed Press, PO Box 7123, Berkeley, CA 94707 USA.

The Contrary Farmer by Gene Logsdon, paperback, 288 pp.
The Contrary Farmer's Invitation to Gardening, by Gene Logsdon, paperback, 180 pp., Chelsea Green. A Gardening Alliance book.

Designing and Maintaining Your Edible Landscape Naturally by Robert Kourik, paperback, Metamorphic Press, 1986.

Drip Irrigation for Every Landscape and All Climates: Helping Your Garden Flourish, While Conserving Water! by Robert Kourik and Heidi Schmidt (Illustrator), paperback, 118 pp., Metamorphic Press, 1983.

Forest Gardening : Cultivating an Edible Landscape by Robert Hart, paperback, 256 pp., Chelsea Green, 1996.

How to Grow More Vegetables: Fruits, Nuts, Berries, Grains, and Other Crops by John Jeavons, 5th ed., paperback, Ten Speed Press, 1995.

Introduction to Permaculture by Bill Mollison and Reny Mia Slay, paperback, 224 pp., Ten Speed Press, 1997.

Lazy-Bed Gardening : The Quick and Dirty Guide by John Jeavons, Carol Cox, Sue Ellen Parkinson (Illustrator), paperback, Ten Speed Press, 1992.

Square Foot Gardening: A New Way to Garden in Less Space With Less Work, by Mel Bartholomew, paperback, 347 pp., Rodale Press, 1985.

Worms Eat My Garbage: How to Set Up and Maintain a Worm Composting System, Mary Appelhof, paperback, Flowerfield Enterprises, 2d ed. 1996.

___The Narrow Way Character Curriculum
A 300 page Eurobound book, including 8 Kingdom Stories ($32.95 plus $3 shipping)

___Volume 1 (Contains 8 Character Building Stories) $16.50
The Governor's Plot (Homeschooling)
The House the World Built (Public Education)
The Alchemist (women & Children at Home)
The Viewing Box (Television & Entertainment)
You Can't Shoot the Bears (Animal Rights?)
The New Command (Loving others)
The Conquered Village (Denying the World)
The Beauty (Inner Beauty vs. Outward)

___Volume 2 (Contains 8 Character Building Stories) - $16.50
The King's Request (Perseverance)
The Goal (Work)
The Love of the King (Obedience)
The Bicycle (Materialism vs. Responsibility)
The Governor's Revenge (Socialization)
The Journey (Following God, Not Men)
The Man of the King (Relationship with God)
The Messenger (Regarding Outward Appearances)

___Volume 3 (Contains 8 Character Building Stories) - $16.50
The King (The Word)
I'll Always have Tomorrow (Procrastination)
The Kite (Blaming Others for our Own Mistakes)
The Fisherman (Being Fishers of Men)
The Baby Cow (Contentment)
The Treasure (True Riches)
One Little Weed (Hidden Sin)
The Gentle Warrior (Speaking the Truth in Love)

_____True Womanhood Text & Workbook ~ $28
_____True Womanhood Text only ~ $21.85
True Womanhood Companion Extra Workbook ~ $10.95

Our Hope Chest Series
_____Personal Help for Girls, Vol. 1 ~ $21.85
_____Preparing Your Hope Chest, Vol. 2 ~ $21.85

_____Personal Help for Boys Text & Workbook ~ $28
_____Personal Help for Boys Text Only ~ $21.85
Personal Help for Boys Companion Workbook~ $10.95

_____What the Bible Says About Being a Girl ~ $3.95
_____What the Bible Says About Being a Boy ~ $3.95

NEW!~ Home Economics for Home Schoolers
_____Level One (6 and up) ~ $17.95
_____Level Two (8 and up) ~ $17.95
_____Level Three (10 and up) ~$17.95

Please add 10% of total purchase for shipping. (Overseas add 25% of total for shipping.)

PEARABLES
P.O. Box 272000
Fort Collins, CO 80527

For special sales and discounts visit us at: www.pearables.com